Donal

LEFT OR RIGHT

THE BOGUS DILEMMA

LEFT / OR

Is every modern nation like the tower,
Half dead at the top?

W. B. YEATS, *Blood and the Moon*

LONDON

/RIGHT

THE BOGUS DILEMMA

Samuel Brittan

SECKER & WARBURG

First published in England 1968 by
Martin Secker & Warburg Limited
14 Carlisle Street, London W 1

Copyright © 1968 by Samuel Brittan

S B N: 436 06871 0

Set in 10 on 11 pt Times Roman type
and printed in Great Britain by
The Camelot Press Limited, London and Southampton

CONTENTS

CONTENTS

ACKNOWLEDGMENTS

There are a number of people to whom I am very much indebted. In the first place I am especially grateful to the Editor of the *Financial Times*, Sir Gordon Newton, for his encouragement and also for the time and facilities he placed at my disposal during an extremely difficult and busy period. Particular thanks are due to friends on whom the manuscript was inflicted. Mr Jonathan Radice and my brother, Leon Brittan, read a very early and fragmentary draft with that combination of encouragement and criticism which I so much needed at the time. At a somewhat later stage, Dr Anthony King and Mr Nigel Lawson generously allowed me to bombard them with vast masses of manuscript at very short notice. If I have still gone off the rails it was not for want of trying on their part. Dr King was also of great assistance as a discriminating guide to the academic literature. Mr Norman Lamont carried out some useful research and made some helpful suggestions on some of the chapters. Miss Diddy Seyd aided me with some valuable enquiries. But apart from these specific obligations, I am grateful to a number of other people with whom I have discussed over a considerable period some of the ideas discussed in this essay.

Thanks are also due to Mr W. Kuhnberg, the *Financial Times* librarian, who found the most obscure references for me at very short notice. But the person who made this book possible was Mrs Anne Shotts, who typed from manuscript which would have made many others give up in despair. National Opinion Polls kindly gave me permission to make use of some of their data for recent years, and acknowledgments are due to Routledge and Kegan Paul and Professor H. J. Eysenck for permission to reproduce Chart 5. I am also grateful to *The Political Quarterly* for allowing me to make use of some paragraphs which originally appeared in an article in the April 1968 issue.

INTRODUCTION

In studying this subject we must be content if we attain as high a degree of certainty as the matter of it permits. The same accuracy or finish is not to be looked for in all discussions any more than in all the productions of the studies and the workshop.

ARISTOTLE, *Ethics*

ONE APPARENTLY SIMPLE ASSUMPTION underlies a great deal of political argument, reporting and analysis. This is, in David Butler's words, 'that political positions can be explained in terms of a spectrum running from extreme left to extreme right and that everyone can be classified in terms of his particular place on that spectrum.'[1]

In the passage just cited Mr Butler goes on to say: 'A man may be to the left on some issues and to the right on others, while in relation to many issues the terms "left" and "right" are meaningless.' My main object in this essay is to argue that these qualifications have now become so important that the left–right spectrum today obscures more than it illuminates. Political discussion, and perhaps even the conduct of politics, would accordingly benefit if it were used much less frequently. For not only is the spectrum concept misleading as a classification of political differences, but its persistence in current discussion has a positively harmful effect. It leads, as I hope to show, to the muffling of important issues, to a bias in favour of certain viewpoints against others, and to the erection of unnecessary barriers between those who should be natural allies.

It would be futile to attempt to ban terms so well established as 'left' and 'right' from political discourse. Like most overworked terms they still have their uses. There are particular issues, mostly centring around the concept of 'equality,' to which they can even now be applied, and there are also unified political attitudes which can legitimately be called 'extreme left' and 'extreme right.' My main attack is concentrated on the idea of a continuous spectrum on which all political attitudes are supposed to be classifiable.

One of the questions I had to ask at the outset was whether I was preaching to the already converted. There is clearly some recognition by politicians and political writers that the left–right spectrum no longer fits the facts exactly. Nevertheless, fear of being placed in the wrong part of the imagined spectrum still inhibits political action; and although writers use expressions such as 'new left,' they use them not as steps on the road to a new classification, but in an attempt to patch up the old. Moreover we have been so used to seeing the political world through left–right spectacles that it is worth making a conscious effort both to examine the resulting distortions and to view the landscape through alternative spectacles (plain glass does not exist).

No British discussion of 'left' and 'right' can go very far without encountering the massive realities of the Labour and Conservative Parties, if only because the political battle tends to concentrate on those issues which can still be put in left–right terms. Anyone who is sufficiently unhappy about the left–right classification to write a book on it is therefore also likely to doubt whether the Labour–Conservative battle reflects the really important divisions of opinion in the country. This lack of correspondence might not matter under some other system, or if British politics were to develop in certain new ways, but it does in present circumstances. Indeed, another reason why I have written this essay is a hope that my own difficulty in choosing between the two main parties may not just be a personal problem, but may raise issues of wider interest.

Limits must, of course, be put on this aspect of the discussion. It is one thing to query whether the traditional vocabulary of political debate adequately expresses the real divisions of opinion; it is quite another thing to bring about a realignment of parties. One can hardly hope to accomplish from an armchair what Mr Grimond tried and failed to achieve from his position as Leader of the Liberal Party. All one can try to do is indicate one or two possible lines of development in British politics which might bring into political discussion more of the real arguments of the day and reduce the amount of shadow-boxing where there is no real conflict of opinion.

This book is an essay and makes no claim to scholarship or original research. In writing it I have been very conscious of important areas either omitted altogether, or dealt with superficially. Above all I regret that lack of time has prevented me from making a comparative study of other Western countries, although I have put up a few signposts here and there. It is conventional at this stage to hope that future authors will be stimulated to more thorough investigations. Such an outcome would indeed be flattering. But I would not have ventured into print if I did not believe that there were certain things that needed saying quickly even at the cost of approximation and imperfection.

The gap between writing and publication always poses problems for a writer on current affairs. The issues mentioned as examples will be just as valid whether they come from the present or the recent past. But I must ask for the reader's indulgence if the tense is wrong. If, as a result of policy changes on either side, the Vietnam War is no longer a current issue by publication date the remarks made in the text about the alignment of British opinion on the war, or on the general merits of the original US venture, will not have lost their illustrative value.

It is of course a risky experiment for someone whose own special knowledge is restricted to the economic field to embark on a political essay at all. In the following pages I have not consciously sought to reduce the risks by concentrating on economic illustrations. On the other hand such illustrations naturally occur more frequently than they would with a different author. On this aspect of the matter—as distinct from the lack of time for more research—I do not feel at all apologetic. The treatment of current affairs in books and newspapers is so dominated by discussion of economic issues by political writers that some comment on political issues from an economic background may help redress the balance.

A brief guide to the plan of the book may be useful. The first chapter attempts to set the scene with a few examples of the left–right confusion. Chapter 2 discusses the historical origins of 'left' and 'right' and the views of a number of writers who believe that they are still relevant. Chapter 3 looks at the actual alignments of voters and politicians to ascertain the residue of meaning that 'left' and 'right' still possess. After that Chapter 4 attempts to spell out the specific harm done by the excessive use of this terminology, and Chapter 5 gives a few tentative suggestions for alternative classifications. There then follow in Chapter 6 a few general observations on the party dialogue. Chapter 7 is a more personal one which discusses the dilemma of a liberal attempting to choose between Labour and Conservative. The final chapter outlines some possible lines of development in British politics which might lead to an improvement on the present situation. It is in no sense a 'conclusion.' The nearest approach to a summary of my criticisms of left and right is in Chapter 4.

It is only fair to warn readers that parts of Chapters 2, 3 and, especially, 5, may be heavier going than the rest of this essay. Those who are mainly interested in my general political observations may prefer to leave these chapters until after the rest of the essay.

Before embarking on my main argument, I cannot, however, resist a short preliminary digression on the role of value judgments in a study of this kind. There is, I am convinced, a hard core of objections to the left–right spectrum, which applies almost irrespective of personal political opinions. Nevertheless it will soon be obvious that I have made no attempt to purge even the descriptive and analytical chapters of this essay from personal value judgments. This is deliberate. For a subsidiary motive for writing this essay is a feeling of dissatisfaction with the way in which too many political analysts, whether in the academic world or the press, attempt to abdicate from all evaluation, almost as a professional principle. Although we are nowadays deluged with books and articles on politics, there is astonishingly little argument on an adult level about the relative merits of the two parties or the tendencies within them. Elections are analysed; the movement of public opinion is studied, and the tactical problems facing the rival leaders are exhaustively discussed. By contrast, expositions or discussions of political viewpoints, at other than the level of party propaganda, are extremely few and far between. Books such as Douglas Jay's *The Socialist Case* or Quintin Hogg's *The Case for Conservatism* seem to belong to a bygone age. Most political writing which is concerned to advocate at all is written for committed partisans whose basic political allegiance can be taken for granted.

The same tendency is noticeable in private conversation. When people of different views meet, arguments are usually about what will happen to their respective parties, not what should. It seems to be regarded as a sign of maturity on such occasions to discuss the problems of the other side with clinical detachment. After a television appearance of Mr Wilson or Mr Heath, the fireside discussion is nearly always on its sales appeal for others, hardly ever on whether what the Leader has said is right or not. As knowledge and sophistication spread, more and more people are trying to predict each other's reactions and fewer and fewer are willing to own up to a genuine reaction of their own. Political allegiances are regarded as an accident, as a matter of convenience, or as a highly personal matter about which it would be as indecent to argue as probing into sex habits would have seemed in the 1880s.

Yeats' well-known lament in *The Second Coming* that 'The best lack all conviction, while the worst/Are full of passionate intensity' is not quite accurate as a description of our society, but it is almost a canon of good behaviour to act as if it were. The fashion for detached and uncommitted political discussion has its uses. It is a protection against the excesses of zeal and fanaticism. It provides a safety valve by which people of different persuasions engaged in public life can engage in civilised intercourse without engaging in non-stop disputes over fundamentals or forced attempts to talk about the latest Test score. Nevertheless the cool, detached approach has dangers of its own. For as the politically educated come to concentrate more and more on organisation, political market research and technical evaluation of party performance, the actual debate on the merits of men and measures descends to a lower and lower level.

This is a real loss. The examination of the strong points and defects of alternative political outlooks, parties and individuals is at least as intellectually demanding an occupation as the analysis and prediction of what is actually going to happen. In the former case we are, in Plato's words, 'discussing no trivial matter, but how we ought to live'—or many aspects of it at least. (The anti-totalitarian claim for an area of personal privacy in which political considerations will not intrude is itself a political position.)

A self-denying ordinance on the part of analysts and commentators is often justified on the grounds that what *ought* to happen is a matter of personal judgment about which intellectual argument is fruitless. An enormous amount of harm has been done by this piece of oversimplified philosophy. As usually presented it suffers from the following weaknesses.

1. The distinction between the two kinds of utterances is a much more subtle one than is realised by those who most loudly proclaim their allegiance to 'positive' studies devoid of value-judgments. Most supposedly factual assertions or descriptions contain some prescriptive or evaluative element; and many apparent value-judgments contain a descriptive element. This is particularly so in the social sciences.

Examples are legion. Nearly all supposedly descriptive words in politics automatically carry with them a strong element of praise or blame. One need only think of the notorious examples such as democratic, liberal or authoritarian. It is also true of the two concepts dealt with in this book, 'left' and 'right'—although their evaluative meanings differ widely in different countries and among different groups. Professor Charles Taylor has had no difficulty in showing how American political scientists who imagine they are abstaining completely from value-judgments are drawn into using explanatory categories, such as the degree to which a society is juridical or tyrannical, which are heavily value-laden.[2] Even if one tried to invent a new and neutral terminology, designated by algebraic symbols, it is almost certain that the value loading would re-emerge by the time the reader had learnt to use them.

Examples of words which are primarily evaluative, but also have a descriptive element, are not quite so frequent, but certainly exist. 'Sound,' 'responsible,' 'enlightened,' are a few that spring to mind. The temptation to use them ironically and in quotation marks is itself suggestive of their descriptive associations. An author is more likely to reduce bias if he tries to be as conscious as possible of the inevitable coexistence of the descriptive and evaluative elements in the terms he uses than if he imagines that he can employ a value-free terminology.

2. Admittedly no philosopher can prove from first principles how men ought to behave in politics or any other sphere. In the last analysis, as Hume pointed out long ago, no 'ought' proposition can be derived from an 'is' statement. Nevertheless people can and do argue about what ought to happen; and they argue not merely about means but about what appear to be ends. This

happens because the last analysis can be a long way off and a good deal of argument is possible before it is reached. Whether Britain should attempt to preserve a specially close relationship with the USA may ultimately be dependent on value-judgments about which no further argument is possible. But a great deal of investigation and analysis is needed before such terminal judgments are reached. The question is every bit as intellectually demanding and respectable as a straightforward investigation of the 'effects' of trying to maintain such a relationship, 'effects' which probably cannot be listed in entirely value-free language, however hard the analyst tries.

The issue has been well summarised by Peter Laslett and W. G. Runciman in their Introduction to the Third Series of papers on *Philosophy, Politics and Society* when they reaffirm the fact–value distinction, but nevertheless insist that prescriptive discussion of political issues is not meaningless, and that both deductive argument and empirical evidence can be brought to bear on it. The view that there can be division of labour, with politicians providing 'value judgments' and experts then telling them how to realise them, has proved to be dangerous nonsense in economic policy-making. The politician would have to know as much as the expert to appreciate where the value judgments come in and what kind are called for. Moreover what passes for a value-judgment in these matters—for example a preference for free enterprise—is usually an instrumental principle which the holder, if he were sane, would be prepared to modify in the light of further knowledge.

3. A writer on politics or economics may well do better if he does not attempt too austere a neutrality, even if his aim is entirely to advance knowledge and not at all to influence events or express opinions. An investigation of what policy-makers 'ought' to do can often act as a most useful tin-opener for uncovering the most coldly objective facts. It happens to be the case that nearly all the great economists from Adam Smith to Keynes started out with strong views on the objects of public policy which motivated their researches and permeated their work. This did not prevent their reaching results which would be equally valid for people of different persuasions. For example, although Keynes was a passionate advocate of full employment, Keynesian techniques can be and have been used to increase the margin of jobless.

Today more insight into the workings of the housing market is likely to come from a researcher who is trying to find out whether rent controls ought to be ended, than from a more detached observer with no such object in mind. It can be shown in some detail that the scientific success of economic forecasts cannot be assessed in isolation from the needs of policy-makers.[3]

Instead of embarking on a sterile quest for a value-free social science, it is usually more profitable to follow out arguments and enquiries wherever they lead, leaving it to others (or to oneself) to ask at the end: 'How much of this depends on the author's purely personal beliefs and how much are we required to accept as a result of his investigations and arguments?'

April 1968

1 / THE LEFT–RIGHT CONFUSION

Man is a creature who lives not upon bread alone, but principally by catchwords.

ROBERT LOUIS STEVENSON, *Virginibus Puerisque*

THE AIM OF THE EXAMPLES PRESENTED in this chapter is to illustrate in a general way the confusion caused by the indiscriminate use of the left–right spectrum. This will set the scene for the argument of later chapters. The examples are mostly taken from the period in 1967–8 when this essay was being prepared. But just as many illustrations could have been supplied from earlier years, and many more will doubtless be available by the time the essay is in the reader's hands.

A recurrent feature of political reporting during the three years following the Labour election victory in 1964 was a sense of mild surprise that left- and right-wing politicians were no longer acting in character. The fact was observed both in connection with the actions of the Labour Government, and even more in relation to the behaviour of 'left' and 'right' within the two political parties. Ian Trethowan, writing in *The Times* early in 1967,[1] remarked that 'Mr Mayhew, Mr Wyatt and Mr Joel Barnett, who by no stretch of the imagination could normally be described as on the left . . . question the cost of defence partly on economic grounds, but also in terms of military reality, particularly East of Suez.' The point presumably was that Labour MPs who did not attract to themselves the label 'left' were taking up what were popularly supposed to be 'left-wing' attitudes.

The critics included the traditional opponents of defence spending among the Labour Party, whom the commentators felt had a proprietary right to the label 'left'; but they also included others in the Parliamentary Labour Party, who had in the past been branded as right or even extreme right, together with a group of Conservative MPs, whose leader, Enoch Powell, was regarded as well to the right, even of the right-wing political party. Against them was ranged what Ronald Butt labelled in the *Financial Times* a 'consensus' embracing both front benches which maintained that Britain 'must maintain its world role—including East of Suez.'[2]

The debates on economic policy provide many further illustrations. Labour MPs who enjoyed the label 'left-wing' disliked intensely the freeze and rising unemployment which followed Mr Wilson's measures of July 1966. But in the 1967 Budget Debate the pioneering call for devaluation as an alternative came from Austen Albu, an ex-Minister always regarded as on the right, and as the year wore on he was joined in his demand by some of the right-wingers prominent in the defence rebellion. Devaluation only became an important 'left-wing' cause just before and after it actually happened. Within the Cabinet, Mr Wilson's staunchest opponents during the period when the preservation of the pound was the main objective of policy were believed to be men such as Roy Jenkins and Anthony Crosland, Mr Gaitskell's former allies in the battles over Clause 4. The supposedly right-wing George Brown was converted to devaluation in the summer of 1965, long before the more 'left-wing' Harold Wilson.

When devaluation actually occurred, it seemed to restore a conventional alignment on economic issues along party lines, with the Labour Party solidly for, and the Conservatives solidly against. But this rallying of forces was superficial and probably temporary. The extent to which views on this range of issues, at once technical and emotional, cut across right–left lines was revealed by the fact that an 'expansionist' manifesto, opposing orthodox deflationary policies had been signed by fourteen Conservative MPs led by David Howell in October 1967, a month before devaluation. Although this group was not prepared to draw the logical conclusion from its attitudes, and refused to recommend a change in the parity, it was more opposed to the orthodox reliance on demand restraint and 'redeployment' than were many loyalist Labour MPs.

Some Conservatives had gone further and flirted with the idea of devaluation and floating rates, even though floating could only be downwards, when the majority of the Labour Cabinet was still solidly against any tampering with the pound. This fact was concealed both by the partisan attractions of opposing the

Government's last-minute change of policy, and also by Mr
Heath's passionate personal opposition to the whole idea of
exchange-rate changes, which made it advisable for dissenters to
lie low. I have no wish to underplay the fact that those who
questioned the parity constituted a select minority and that the
emotional heart even of the Parliamentary Conservative Party,
let alone of the Party in the constituencies, was outraged at
devaluation. The nature of the emotions that govern the Conservative attitudes will have to be discussed later in this essay.
My point here simply is that among the few who understood and
had thought about the matter, attitudes cut across both party
lines and right–left divisions within the Parties.

The fact that exchange-rate changes were advocated by many
staunch anti-socialists with a strong belief in the capitalist system
is even more obvious if one glances at the academic world. One
critic right outside the British Isles called for a move, not to
another fixed parity but to a floating rate, remarking that 'it
would be bitterly opposed by foreign central bankers, whose
elaborate support mechanisms would be made unnecessary and
their egos deflated accordingly.' Was this a frustrated left-wing
Labour MP letting off steam, or an article in *Tribune*? In fact
these words were written in a *Sunday Telegraph* symposium[3] by
Professor Milton Friedman, the head of the Chicago School of
economists, who has always been regarded as an extreme right-
wing economist on account of his devotion to the market economy
and who went so far as to assist Senator Goldwater in his 1964
Presidential campaign.* The same line was proclaimed in a
pamphlet by Enoch Powell. Equally significantly, it was the more
'left-wing' of the Labour Government's economic advisers, who
took longest to come round to devaluation. (Dr Thomas Balogh,
who was Mr Wilson's personal economic adviser, twice wrote
to *The Times* in 1961 and 1963 denouncing the whole idea.)

In Britain some Socialists had been reluctant for a long time
to press for devaluation because they believed that the real 'left-
wing' alternative to Mr Wilson's earlier reliance on deflation

---

* In this Professor Friedman himself fell victim to the right–left mythology.
At least one of his former pupils, well aware that Professor Friedman's own
views spring from a deep devotion to individual liberty, was sad to see him
take at face value the economic language of a crude, illiberal jingoist and
militarist.

would have been a permanent statutory incomes policy. This seemed for example the view of Mr Crossman, who was often regarded as on the left of the Cabinet, after July 1966. Yet at that time those Labour M Ps who opposed even the Government's own temporary prices and incomes restraints were continually described in the Press as the 'hard core' of left-wing irreconcilables. Thus both extreme support for, and extreme hostility to, a compulsory incomes policy could apparently serve as a criterion for being on the left. As 'left-wing' and 'socialist' were 'hurrah' words they could be used for almost any policy by the person bestowing the label: incomes regulation or an industrial free-for-all, a preference for Europe, for the Commonwealth or for 'going it alone', and support for either side in the Arab-Israeli dispute. The bitter split in the ranks of the Labour Left over the 1967 Middle Eastern war was in fact not an isolated episode, but a dramatic illustration of how difficult it was becoming on more and more issues to decide which position should be labelled left-wing.

One can go on indefinitely multiplying instances. Roy Jenkins was for a long time regarded as on the far right of the Labour Party and so, to about the same degree, was Miss Alice Bacon. But, judging by press accounts, the relationship between them, when Mr Jenkins was Home Secretary and Miss Bacon Minister of State, was far from happy. For Mr Jenkins being on the right wing meant a tolerant attitude towards the capitalist element in a mixed economy, a permissive attitude towards personal behaviour, and a somewhat unproletarian social life. For Miss Bacon being on the right meant a stout defence of traditional values together with a censorious attitude towards the rich and their doings.

If a prominent Conservative illustration is required, one need only recall the ambiguity of Mr Macmillan's position in the spectrum. He was brought to power by those who were regarded as being on the Party's right; yet in office he alienated traditionalists by his rapid liquidation of colonial commitments and his dramatic switch towards Europe, while at home he became identified with full employment, even at the risk of inflation, and in his last years of office he made 'economic planning' respectable again. Some reviewers of his autobiography have attacked him for having been a 'socialist' all the time, but the whole tone of his Government, with its record number of Dukes, Earls and Peers and the proliferation of newly created baronetcies, hardly conjured up left-wing associations. Nor did his role in the selection of Sir Alec Douglas-Home as his successor or his selection of men for Cabinet posts before the 1962 purge.

Not surprisingly the concept of the centre is as confused as that of the left and right, between which it is supposed to lie. In the Nuffield study of the 1964 election, Butler and King[4] refer to the very real possibility that the so-called centre voter can exhibit extremist attitudes, for example on immigration. Thus whatever else the defining characteristics of the centre are, they do not necessarily include the avoidance of extremes.

According to the conventional classification, however, it is the Liberals who are in the centre (although this must be a very different centre from that referred to in the Nuffield study). Nevertheless, after Jeremy Thorpe's election as leader of the Liberal Party one Labour MP privately remarked that the Liberals were now 'further to the left than the majority of the Labour Party.' There was, however, some argument about whether this was true. One disgruntled Liberal is said to have remarked 'Jeremy only looks more left-wing because he talks about Africa.'[5]

Attempts to use the left–right spectrum outside the Western political context are even more likely to run aground. Victor Zorza once reported that the divisions of opinion among Soviet Leaders, between those who believed in seeking common ground with the USA and the hardliners who believe in unremitting hostility, were seen in Washington as a conflict between right and left.[6] Mr Zorza rightly regards this as an improvement on the earlier Washington view of the Communist World as a monolithic evil. But which of the Soviet factions should be regarded as left, and which right? On the Western analogy, it is tempting to regard the more pacific party as being on the left. On the other hand, it has traditionally been the left wing of the Communist movement which has stood for world revolution and was once denounced by Lenin for its pains in a book entitled *Left-Wing Communism: An Infantile Disorder*. (The margin between an infantile left-winger and a Fascist beast can at times be a narrow one.) One wonders what is gained from introducing the concepts at all. If simplified labels are required, surely the 'hawk–dove' classification, also mentioned by Zorza, is preferable for issues of this kind?

Even this superficial selection of illustrations shows that in recent years left-wingers and right-wingers have been behaving uncharacteristically and that politicians' positions on many issues seem to bear less and less relation to where they might appear on a spectrum diagram. The situation becomes even more confusing when diametrically opposed attitudes seem to have equal claim to be labelled 'left' or 'right.' If individuals belie their beliefs too frequently and many issues cannot be fitted into the classification at all, the classification itself is severely called into question.

Before leaving these preliminary examples, let us consider a seemingly far-fetched case, the characters in *Don Giovanni*. The Commendatore is clearly a right-wing authority figure. But how about Don Giovanni himself? His rebellion against authority and the conventions might suggest he is on the left. On the other hand his contemptuous attitude towards the poor, represented by Masetto, his unquestioning assumption of the right to privileged treatment, and the overtones of the feudal *droit de seigneur*, rule out any such categorisation. Indeed he could have expected the same type of denunciation from the egalitarians and the opponents of privilege as 'property speculators' and 'take-over-bidders' received in the period before the 1964 election. Who then represents the left? Is it the unfortunate Masetto, the good proletarian, humiliated, beaten and ridiculed, not aspiring to change his station, but determined not to let the Don get away with anything 'unfair'?

The *Don Giovanni* example brings out in a more illuminating way than many all-night sittings some of the ambiguities inherent in the left–right distinction. *Fidelio*, a slightly later opera, illustrates on the other hand the historical moment when the distinction was clear and meaningful. There the conflict is between tyrannical authority and freedom. It represents the mood of the storming of the Bastille when for one brief instant reason, liberty, equality, humanity and justice all seemed united on the side of the French Revolution. Indeed the whole left–right dichotomy is a product of that Revolution; as we shall see in the next chapter, the later anomalies arose from the attempt to force subsequent political argument into the mould of 1789 when that mould was no longer appropriate.

2 / WORDS AND IDEAS

Perhaps the plaintive numbers flow
For old, unhappy, far-off things,
And battles long ago:

WORDSWORTH, *The Solitary Reaper*

THE ORIGIN OF THE TERMS LEFT AND RIGHT goes back to the first meetings of the French States-General in 1789, when the nobility took the place of honour on the King's right while the ordinary members—'The Third Estate'—sat on the King's left. Although there are other versions of this particular episode, there is little doubt that at a very early stage the more revolutionary deputies were sitting on the left of the Assembly and the more conservative ones on the right. The division of opinion along these lines first became explicit in the debates on the Royal Veto. The Right favoured an absolute veto, the Left was against any veto, and a Centre emerged which favoured the compromise of a suspensive veto.

It is less well known that these terms are comparatively late arrivals on the British scene. The first recorded use in Britain of 'left' and 'right' in a political context is given by the Oxford English Dictionary as Carlyle's *French Revolution*, published in 1837. The terms were slow to take root and they did not come into general currency in this country until the 1920s.[1] Even today they occupy a very minor place in most English and American text-books on political thought and are not mentioned at all in many standard volumes.

The fact that they are fairly recent imports from the Continent may, together with their abstract nature, help to explain why they have almost no meaning for the mass of the voting public. The forthcoming Nuffield study of the 'British Voter' by Stokes and Butler is expected to show that most of the electorate have not the faintest idea of what is implied by these terms. Despite their constant use in the press and on television, 'left' and 'right' are still elite words, which have meaning only for the small politically interested minority. Philip Converse has already shown that less than a fifth of a recent electoral sample in the USA had a reasonably accurate understanding of the partially analogous American 'liberal-conservative' dichotomy and about half the sample were completely confused about its meaning.[2] In France, as one would expect, public opinion surveys seem to show more reaction to the left–right labels.

Despite their remoteness from most electors 'left' and 'right' are far from being neutral descriptions, but are highly emotive terms for those who use them. The nature of the coveted position has varied at different times and in different places. Originally to be on the right was a mark of honour. 'Our language tends to assess right as superior, worthier and morally preferable to left', according to the anthropologist, James Littlejohn.[3] 'While many men would be pleased to be considered upright,' he remarks, 'few are happy to receive a left-handed compliment.' This dualism is frequently found in primitive, as well as advanced societies. Mr Littlejohn has remarked that 'the Nuer of the Sudan classify under right: men, good, strength, life, east; and under left: women, evil, weakness, death, west.'

In the Bible too, left symbolises bad and the right good; the goats were placed on the left in the Gospel of St Matthew. The use of one word for right-hand and right in the ethical sense is no coincidence and occurs in several languages. Very often the right side conjured up an image of might and right in harmonious association. Christ is envisaged in the Gospels as sitting on the right hand of God and this is emphatically reasserted in both the *Gloria* and *Credo* of the Mass. Nobody who has heard the chorus thundering out the words 'qui sedes ad dexteram Patris' in Beethoven's *Missa Solemnis* is likely to forget the symbolism. It was thus more than mere chance that the place of honour in the French Assembly of 1789 was on the King's right. In the United States the old symbolism has to some extent remained. While the centre is probably regarded as conjuring up more favourable associations than the right, a 'leftist' label is a mark of opprobrium which most politicians would go a long way to avoid.

On this side of the Atlantic the emotive content of the two terms is very different. As a result of the identification of the right with the anti-popular side at the time of the French Revolution, a reversal of emotional associations occurred. In Europe, and above all in France, the coveted political label has been 'left-wing.' This has been so much so that conservative French parties have been accustomed to carry labels such as Left Republicans and Democratic Left, and the reluctance to occupy the right-wing benches in the Assembly has led to serious disputes. As William Pickles remarks in his perceptive contribution on the topic in the *Dictionary of the Social Sciences*, 'the term "right" is most commonly (though not exclusively) used as a pejorative term, by those who believe themselves to be on the left.'

The asymmetrical nature of the two terms is vividly illustrated by a good standard text by a group of American scholars, entitled *The European Right*,[4] which is mostly devoted not to the moderate anti-socialist parties, but to the extreme right including the Nazis, the Falangists, and Admiral Horthy's regime in Hungary. Another fascinating example occurred not very long ago when one of the brightest luminaries among French conservatives, M. Giscard d'Estaing, was most reluctant to speak to a club of younger British Tories for fear of being associated with a 'right-wing gathering.'

In Britain today, there is little doubt that the favourite place to be is 'just left of centre.' Labour Prime Ministers like to think of themselves as slightly to the left of centre in the general political spectrum, but also 'just left of centre' within their own party. (The incompatibility of the two positions from the point of view of the spectrum theory has never seemed to cause anxiety.) Attlee's secret was said to be that he led the Labour Party from 'left of centre'— incredible though this may seem from his record. Although Harold Wilson was more usually described as plain 'centre' during his honeymoon period with the political commentators, he has nevertheless publicly expressed his admiration for Attlee's stance, and has been ready to nourish the lingering belief of his old Bevanite associates that his heart is really on the left.

A Conservative Prime Minister also aims to be 'left of centre' in terms of his own party spectrum. Most commentators willingly accorded Mr Macmillan this accolade. Even those Conservative Ministers with the most unbending public image, such as Selwyn Lloyd or the then Mr Henry Brooke, would have indignantly denied that they were anywhere near the right wing of the party. When Sir Alec Douglas-Home was asked what sort of Conservative he regarded himself as, he duly replied 'left of centre.'

Kingsley Amis has attempted to reverse normal associations and create a transatlantic pattern by coining the repellent term 'Lefty.'[5] But at no time in the post-war period has right, or even 'right of centre,' been an attractive label. The far left of the spectrum, as represented by the left of the Labour Party has, it is true, often had an unfavourable image, but the acceptable range has never deviated far from the area between the centre and the moderate left.

The strong evaluative element in the terms also emerges from the arguments given by some authors, which are examined below, to justify the continued importance of the left–right dichotomy. For they are often not merely arguments for a particular descriptive classification, but also arguments for taking up a left-wing position. There may at one time have been a genuine preference on the part of the politically vocal public for distinguishable policies which could be meaningfully labelled as 'left,' but not 'extreme left.' As a result left and right may linger on as terms of praise and blame, even if preferences have changed, and the terms have lost most of their meaning. Such a shift from a predominantly descriptive to a predominantly evaluative meaning is common-place in the history of language. (It is the converse of the process described by R. M. Hare in *The Language of Morals*, Oxford 1952, by which evaluative words degenerate into descriptive terms, often used ironically in quotation marks.)

As left and right originated in France and did not come into widespread use in this country until well into the twentieth century, a glance at French experience is necessary to understand the way their use developed and changed. We have already seen how the French Assembly of 1789–91 split into left, centre, and right on the issue of the Royal Veto. A similar division showed itself on other issues, especially the franchise. The restricted franchise was challenged in the name of popular sovereignty by Robespierre and the 'Left,' while other leaders ranging from the Right to the Left Centre were prepared to accept it. A further split opened up between the Jacobins and the extreme Left, such as the Enragés, who wanted day-by-day popular control of the Government by the Parisian 'masses.' Robespierre himself did not believe in representative democracy in the modern sense, but wished directly to enforce Rousseau's 'general will' without the corruption of intermediaries. Professor Talmon has described in detail the thought processes by which the most fanatical believers in popular sovereignty, for whom parliamentary representation was too imperfect an instrument, became the apostles of a minority dictatorship.[6]

After the Bourbon Restoration of 1815 political classifications still referred back to the French Revolution. The Left were the supporters, not necessarily of the Jacobin excesses of 1793–4, but of the 'spirit of 1789.' The Left were above all else republicans, the Right monarchists who were themselves divided between the supporters of the Bourbons, the Orléanists and the Bonapartists. In nineteenth-century France anti-clericalism became closely linked with republicanism as a left-wing cause. Until the turn of the century, the threats to the Republic posed by the Church and the Army, as well as opposition to the anti-semitism that came to the fore in the Dreyfus affair, united the left irrespective of attitudes to socialism.

Indeed the advance of socialist doctrines on the French left was a very slow process and was never quite complete. It is true that as early as 1798 the conspiracy of Babeuf, who regarded himself with some justification as the successor of Robespierre, aimed to establish a form of distributivist communism. But while the French 'economic left' was vocal throughout the nineteenth century, it was, as David Caute has put it, a 'junior partner' to the political left until the Paris Commune of 1871.[7] Even after the First World War the French Radicals continued to insist that they were part of the left. Despite their opposition to socialism, they took part in the Popular Front from 1935 to 1938 in response to the threat from the neo-Fascist Leagues, and did not finally leave it until after the Blum Government had demanded a capital levy. To make matters more confusing they insisted on calling themselves the *Parti Radical-Socialiste,* which is the one thing they were not.

By the time the term 'left' arrived in Britain after the First World War, Labour had become the main opponent of the Conservatives. The Labour Party had just become committed to a constitution containing the famous Clause 4, which demanded the 'common ownership of the means of production, and the best obtainable system of popular administration and control of each industry.' The British left was then mainly identified with the Labour and Communist parties and smaller Socialist sects. But the identification was never exclusive; and the older Continental association with general liberal and democratic values was never quite lost when the term came into vogue in Britain.

On both sides of the Channel the cry of popular sovereignty was sometimes used to rationalise the new socialist thinking and to connect it with the earlier, more purely political, left-wing tradition. Despite universal franchise, it was argued, sovereignty did not lie with the people so long as the real seats of power were in irresponsible private hands. Even many on the left who would not go as far as this underwent a change in their economic and social doctrines. While the left had originally been the standard-bearer of *laisser-faire*, it ended up as the apostle of state control and public ownership. The sociological explanation for this dramatic switch is that in the early nineteenth century it was the bourgeois middle class who championed the cause of reform and revolution to capture the state from the Crown, Church and aristocracy. Later on the middle class became a conservative force, while with the extension of the franchise the popular movement became dominated by the industrial working classes and their demands.

But any attempt to impose a neat pattern is complicated by the persistence until well into the twentieth century of issues on which the left continued to be more *laisser-faire* than the right, above all that of Free Trade versus tariffs. Even as late as the General Election of 1923, which brought the first Labour Government to office, the main issue was Free Trade on which Labour sided solidly with the Liberals. Moreover even some working-class demands could be presented as libertarian demands for the removal of restraints. It was, for example, the Liberal Government of 1906 which passed the Trade Disputes Act which liberated the unions from the Taff Vale decision.

The complex and contradictory nature of both 'left' and 'right' arises from the coexistence of many different historical layers of meaning. Even today the old associations of 'left' with political and personal freedom, anti-militarism, religious tolerance and general civilised values, and 'right' with their opposites, are not yet dead. This explains in large measure those merchant bankers of London and Paris or the German publishing houses who, despite their obvious personal commitment to capitalism, prefer not to regard themselves as on the right. It is only since the 1950s that the Jewish business community in Britain has been happy to vote for the Conservative Party. Even in France in recent times, a better prediction has been possible of whether a citizen is on the left or the right on the basis of the clerical issue than on class or economic controversies.[8]

The straight identification of the left with opposition to capitalism was in fact only accurate during what Professor Samuel Beer has called the 'socialist generation'—in England from the Labour Party's adoption of the 1918 constitution to about 1950.[9] Since then many 'revisionist' thinkers, above all Hugh Gaitskell and Anthony Crosland, have challenged this interpretation of the meaning of 'left,' and it has gone out of favour both in the British Labour Party and among Continental Social Democrats, even where there has been no formal renunciation. The negative reason for this development has been the discovery that state ownership does nothing to increase workers' control. Indeed, by reducing the number of employers in an industry to one, it increases the monopoly power of management in the labour market.

The positive reason has been the Keynesian Revolution. Governments have found ways of exercising economic sovereignty without the need for ownership, which has become an irrelevant nuisance. By means of their control over the level of demand they have been able to avoid the slumps which were such a curse of pre-war capitalism, and they have acquired considerable power to influence the distribution of economic growth between regions. They also have some—although not unlimited—power to use taxes and social services to change the distribution of income and property. At a more sophisticated level, modern economic analysis has dissolved the crude opposition between 'production for profit' and 'production for use.' Both in Communist Eastern Europe and the British nationalised industries the profit motive has been brought back into play as the best approximate guide to production decisions. The conditions in which the profit motive will lead to beneficial results depend on technical factors—mainly how far the real costs to the community of alternative courses of action can be reflected in money costs and prices—and hardly at all on ownership; the vague drift of this analysis has got through to politicians, if only from the briefs received during their periods in office.

Faced with these changes one can reasonably say that public ownership and a promise to 'abolish capitalism' have ceased to be the distinguishing feature of the left. Numerous alternative candidates have been put in their place—including equality, an attack on the 'class system,' a bias in favour of public spending and a return to the old liberal causes of removing restraint on personal freedom, modernising anachronistic institutions, a special hostility to racial discrimination and more internationalist-minded attitudes abroad. Some fundamentalists would find this interpretation utterly unacceptable and would say with David Caute that large sections of the British Labour Party and European Social Democrats have ceased to be left-wing, and that 'today the left generally begins at some point within these parties.'[10]

This seemingly semantic dispute conceals a deep-seated division of views towards the Welfare Capitalism of the post-war years. Those who are prepared to tolerate it do not *deserve*, in the view of their opponents, the honourable label 'left.' The argument is only possible in these terms because of an ambiguity in the term 'left.' It can be used in opposition to right; it can also be used in the sense of the Labour Left, to describe the more 'extreme' group within the left. Both meanings are in use and neither is any more 'real' than the other.

The evolution of the historical right is much more difficult to trace, partly because of the pejorative overtones of the term. It is not a label that democratic politicians have been at all anxious to assume; and in practice the centre and the right have been defined negatively by the distance of their views from the left.

Again we must start with France. Originally the right consisted of the defenders of the institutions attacked by the French Revolution. They rallied to the support of the established Church and the aristocracy, and later in the nineteenth century they attracted the support of the army, but above all else they were monarchists. In nineteenth-century France they were split into three camps: the Legitimists who supported the Bourbons, the Orléanists and the Bonapartists. Of these the Legitimists were generally regarded as the most unambiguously right-wing. It may come as a shock to those who identify the far right with out-and-out support for business interests that the Legitimists distributed tracts protesting against the shelling of the Lyons proletariat by the 'bourgeois' monarch, Louis-Philippe. This alliance was not entirely opportunist: the Royalist right had in common with the socialist workers a common dislike of bourgeois individualism which they wished to subordinate to 'higher' national values. A similar dream of an alliance between the proletariat and the Crown against the upstart manufacturers inspired the young Disraeli. The pioneer of social insurance in nineteenth-century Europe was not any reformist liberal regime, but Bismarck in Germany.

During the late nineteenth and early twentieth century the protection of capitalism against the threat of socialism did become of increasing importance to the European right. The common thread linking the earlier right-wing championship of Crown, Church and aristocracy to its later concern for capitalist interests was a concern for property—a concept differing considerably in emphasis from the liberal belief in the free market and in removing barriers to enterprise. Yet the primary preoccupations of the Continental right remained surprisingly unchanged, and after 1871 the French Third Republic had to defend itself against a series of monarchist threats.

The end of the nineteenth century saw the birth of a new kind of right wing in Continental politics. Although there are threads linking it with some of the 'ultras' who supported the Bourbons, it could by no stretch of the imagination be regarded as conservative. Whatever romantic inspiration it drew from the myth of an uncorrupted past, it vied with the Marxists in demanding a sweeping overhaul of national life. The expression 'Right' when used without qualification is more frequently applied by writers to this movement than to the more humdrum conservative defenders of the established order. This new right was an attempt to escape from the frustrations of urban and industrial life and to move to a more emotional and physical plane of existence, usually accompanied by intense nationalist feelings. It can be traced in writers such as Nietzsche, Kipling, d'Annunzio or even D. H. Lawrence. It would be absurd to identify these men with the perversion of the gas chambers, even though the Nazi period is a warning of the direction in which these ideas can lead in unscrupulous or unsophisticated hands.

Right-wing movements, in this far-out sense, have supported a good many different beliefs. But one point that is clear is that their economic beliefs were not at the opposite extreme from those of the left. Although they have drawn support from the fears of Communism of the middle class, extreme right-wing movements have normally been hostile to capitalism and to anything approaching economic *laisser-faire*—the name 'National Socialist' is itself revealing. On such questions they have often been nearer to the Socialists and even the Communists than to the orthodox bourgeois parties. In many countries, including Germany, the extreme right offered itself as a radical alternative to Marxism. The Communist and ultra-nationalist movements competed for the loyalties of the same working-class districts—and often of the same action-hungry intellectuals.

In Britain the term right has had a rather negative role. No one has rushed to claim the label; and it has mainly been used by those on the left as a name for their opponents. Some Conservatives have always disliked the description intensely; but by the postwar period there was a tendency to make the best of it and the Party's 1949 manifesto was called 'The Right Road for Britain.'

There has always been an ambiguity in the use of the term right, similar to that found in the case of left. Sometimes 'the right' is used broadly to cover all segments of Conservative and other anti-Socialist opinion. At other times it is used more narrowly to refer to certain extreme groups in the Tory Party and further beyond it. In the inter-war period, the right in this latter sense consisted of two rather different groups: on the one hand the intellectual descendants of the pre-1914 Imperialists and, on the other, those who wanted to introduce in Britain some of the extreme nationalist ideas of the Continental far right. The first, respectable, right was characterised by Churchill's campaign against the India Bill in the 1930s and by Beaverbrook's campaign for Empire Free Trade. The non-respectable right was symbolised by Mosley's Fascists (it is significant that Mosley was originally a Labour MP, who turned to Fascism after he became disillusioned with the refusal of the 1929–31 Labour Government to tackle the unemployment problem).

In the post-war period the near-Fascist right has had no overt political importance, while the imperialists have been fighting a purely defensive losing battle. The present beliefs of the Tory Right will be examined in the next chapter. As 'right' is more a 'boo' word than a 'hurrah' one, there have been no agonising debates in right-wing circles on the correct contemporary meaning of the term, and no disputes about who is truly entitled to use it, as there have been on the left.

There should be little further need to labour the point that left and right have stood for a great many different attitudes in the century and three-quarters since 1789, with much overlapping and internal contradiction. A fuller historical survey would have produced an even more tangled picture. Moreover, many of the classic left–right issues now bear a distinctly dated look and it is far from obvious that they have a direct counterpart on the contemporary scene.

Those political writers who still believe in the validity of the left–right distinction usually interpret it either in terms of attitudes to equality or of attitudes to change. There is little logical reason why there should be any close connection between the two sets of attitudes; and, as we shall see, there is not all that much tendency for them to coincide in practice. One of the leading exponents of the change criterion is the French political scientist Professor Maurice Duverger, who believes that the fundamental political conflict is 'between those who are more or less satisfied with the existing social order and who wish to preserve it, and those whom this order does not suit and who wish to change it.'[11]

This definition will only do on the assumption that the right has been in power most of the time and has had its way (two entirely different assumptions, as the experience of Britain in 1951–64 confirms). To identify the 'left' with change ignores the whole question of what kind of change. This definition would identify the left wing in the Soviet Union with those who wish to restore capitalism. The campaign in Britain in the 1960s for a reduction in surtax was a demand for a change in the existing order, but it was hardly associated with the left! In the USA a Goldwater drive to wind up 'state welfare' and give more power to the military would have meant far more change than Johnson's Great Society.

A different version of the change criterion has been given by Roy Jenkins. Mr Jenkins regards himself as left-wing in the sense that he does not believe in accepting established answers or established positions just because they have always been so accepted. He believes that the party of the left should be 'challenging and optimistic.' It should have 'faith in the constant ability of human society, led in the right direction, to improve on its organisation and values.' The party of the right by contrast is 'pessimistic in the sense of thinking that change is more likely to do harm than good.'[12] This is an excellent summary. But there are still certain problems about the suggested classification. There is no necessary connection between a sceptical attitude towards conventional beliefs and institutions and an optimistic faith in human progress. A person could well be equally sceptical in both directions. The link between reason and political radicalism would have made no sense to some eighteenth-century thinkers, of whom the Tory sceptic David Hume was a notable example. Nor would it make sense to a number of the contemporary dis-illusioned who are equally emancipated from the traditional pieties and from the nineteenth-century belief in progress.

But the greatest difficulty is in linking attitudes to change with the left–right battle in Britain. 'One of the supreme ironies of the 1966 election,' according to the Nuffield study, 'was that the final emphasis of the Conservative leader was on the need for radical change, and of the leader of the Labour party on the need for patriotism and stability.'[13] The Nuffield authors remark that the Conservatives 'were indeed putting forward one of the most radical programmes advanced by any party since the war.' This radicalism admittedly did not touch the first-order problems of Britain's place in the world and the management of the economy. In those areas both parties were in 1966 still stuck in an official cross-bench consensus. But Mr Heath and his closest supporters undoubtedly intended to make the more radical appeal, and in the view of qualified and detached observers they did so. It would be special pleading to explain away the proposed reforms in trade-union law, social security and the tax system, let alone entry into the Common Market, as an attempt 'to return to the past.' Yet it would be equally absurd to say that the Conservatives had become egalitarian. If anything, they had moved in the other direction compared with their position under Macmillan. Thus a definition of left and right in terms of attitudes to change may often be inconsistent with one in terms of attitudes to equality.

In developing his change criterion, Duverger distinguishes between the extreme right, who would oppose all change, and the moderate right, who would accept some limited change. On this basis the theory becomes even less convincing. Even the brief review in these pages of movements to the right of the official Conservative leadership has shown that they have invariably demanded more change rather than less. The Duverger theory cannot be saved by the fact that this change has sometimes been advocated in the name of a return to the virtues of a bygone age. Quite apart from the fact that this claim is not always made—Imperial Union for example, was a new idea with little past—it would be to confuse myth with reality to take it at face value. The very fact that, as Duverger himself emphasies, the 'real left' and the 'real right' have been in power for such very short periods in France makes it probable that both extremes would favour change, while if any vested interests exist against change, they are more likely to be found in the centre (or, in British terms, within the consensus of the two front benches).

The most plausible case that can be made for the continued relevance of left and right hangs not on change at all, but on attitudes to social and economic equality. The continued co-existence of two different political traditions on this subject particularly strikes observers of overseas origin. Professor Blondel identifies these as the working-class ideas of equality and fraternity, and the upper-middle-class concept of hierarchy.[14] Professor Samuel Beer uses almost the same expressions: an egalitarian-democratic ideal on the one hand, and an emphasis on authority and the need for a governing class on the other. He takes for his theme a quotation from *Troilus and Cressida* used by that notable authority-figure Sir John Anderson (later Lord Waverley) in 1947:

> Take but degree away, untune that string,
> And, hark! what discord follows.

He finds in this the continuing theme that separates the two British parties when so many of the old socialist–capitalist arguments have been made obsolete by events.[15]

How far this cleavage with regard to status, hierarchy and authority has been affected by recent changes in the Conservative Party, it is too early to say. Professor Beer has no difficulty in showing that the more 'philosophical' of Tory writers stressed the need for a governing class well into the post-war period. The election of Mr Heath to the Conservative leadership has not eliminated the unspoken identification of the political right with the boarding-school culture, even though the special privileges attaching to this culture may be rapidly diminishing. Moreover, in a slightly different form, ideas of hierarchy and an emphasis on human inequality are even more clearly marked in the non-public school middle classes with their meritocratic values. Indeed the most obvious clash between the two traditions in recent years has been not on the public schools, but the battle between the comprehensive and the grammar schools.

This conflict of values is related to, but is by no means the same as, a much more down-to-earth material conflict between classes. W. G. Runciman calls the latter the sociological distinction: 'nothing other than the perennial argument between rich and poor.' As it stands this definition is loaded against the right. It should be expanded to cover all the manual working class on the one hand and the middle class as well as the rich on the other. Moreover the simple gaining of working-class votes does not make a party left-wing. Nor does a concern for the absolute welfare of the working class, voiced for example by some Tory Democrats. The left is concerned with improving the *relative* position of the poor and the manual working class considered as groups (trade unionists, pensioners, wage earners, rather than individuals) and is hostile to the interests of the relatively better-off. The right by contrast will emphasise national rather than sectional advance, but is particularly concerned with those types of advances which can be brought about by improving, or protecting, the relative position of the middle and upper classes, whether these are businessmen or salaried employees.

Conflicts between the hierarchical and the egalitarian concepts of society, and between middle- and working-class material demands, undoubtedly exist, although rarely in clear-cut form; and they supply whatever residue of meaning may still remain in the left–right labels. But as the following two chapters will argue, this terminology is a badly distorting influence when applied, as it so often is, to the whole of the political scene; and even on class-related issues, it has a constricting and unfortunate effect on the whole debate.

3 / THE CONCEPTS
IN PRACTICE

Tolerably early in life I discovered that one of the unpardonable sins, in the eyes of most people, is for a man to go about unlabelled.

T. H. HUXLEY

THE WAY TO DISCOVER HOW THE TERMS 'left' and 'right' operate in Britain today is to examine empirically the attitudes advanced by those who are given those labels. This is the best recipe for avoiding the fallacy of 'essentialism,' of supposing that words have real meanings known to thinkers, different from and superior to those given to them in their normal application.

The first obstacle to any such examination is that, as indicated in the previous chapter, these terms make little if any impact on the bulk of the electorate. Nor is this merely a matter of lack of familiarity with the actual words. American investigations have shown that there is little connection between the general public's views on one subject and its views on another. One recent investigation by Philip Converse has demonstrated that attitudes to different policy questions among American voters are not organised into belief-systems which would justify attaching to them the transatlantic labels of 'liberal' or 'conservative.' A belief-system is defined as a relation between attitudes, such that if we knew a person's attitude to one set of issues we would have some success in predicting his attitudes to others. For example, if a voter were opposed to a high level of social security payments, we would predict that he was a conservative and probably hostile to trade unions; and we would expect him to hold certain views on foreign policy as well. But much more often than not we should be wrong. For such belief-systems are mainly conspicuous by their absence among the mass electorate.[1]

Apart from the lack of correlation between people's opinions on different policy issues, their reported views on the same issues seem to shift almost at random. When members of Converse's sample were polled at two-yearly intervals over a four-year period, 'only about thirteen people out of twenty managed to locate themselves even on the same *side* of the controversy in successive interrogations when ten out of twenty would have done so by chance alone.' Moreover the greatest instability of all was shown in issues relating to the role of public and private enterprise in housing and utilities—just the type of issue which on both sides of the Atlantic is supposed to characterise the two main rival tendencies.

The 1952 US Presidential election in which Eisenhower swept into power, was widely interpreted as a swing to the right, or in American terms a conservative reaction to two decades of New Deal and Fair Deal. This turns out to be a historical myth. In fact no widespread change in policy views could be located among those sampled. As Angus Campbell has put it, voters were thinking of the 'men in Washington, the stalemate in Korea and General Eisenhower's heroic image. So far from voting for a more conservative programme, only a small percentage had any apparent comprehension of what a conservative–liberal or a left–right dimension in politics implies.'[2]

The indications are that this lack of left or right belief systems holds at least as strongly in Britain as in the USA. Most of the evidence so far published relates opinions on different subjects, not to each other, but to party allegiance; but even here the conclusions are startling enough. In an analysis of British Institute of Public Opinion Polls surveys for 1959–61, Professor Blondel has shown that on a vast range of issues there is almost no connection between beliefs on policy and party allegiance. Support for official policies on nuclear armaments was often no higher among Conservative than Labour voters, even though the nuclear disarmers were supposed to be associated with the Labour Left. A very large majority among supporters of both parties held the heretical view that East Germany should be recognised. There was very little correlation between views on crime and punishment, or on a 'permissive' issue such as licensing law reform, and party allegiance.[3]

More recent investigations have found, if anything, even less relationship between the proclaimed belief-system of the parties and the views of the ordinary public. During the two years 1966–7, the *National Opinion Poll Political Bulletin* showed a fluctuation between a high of just over 50 per cent and a low of 25 per cent

THE CONCEPTS IN PRACTICE

in the proportion of Conservative supporters who thought
Britain should back the USA in Vietnam. Yet during this period
official Conservative policy was to go 'all the way with L.B.J.'
Even on questions such as Rhodesia, on which there were extremely
strong and divergent feelings among Labour and Conservative
activists, opinion among NOP's electoral sample was at best
marginally related to party allegiance.

The only way of employing the terms left and right in connection with the mass electorate is to relate them, not to ideological
beliefs, but to voting behaviour. This will be called for convenience
the 'weak' sense of the left and right. To say that someone is on
the right is then defined to mean that he is more likely to vote
Conservative than Labour and vice versa. Liberals, 'don't knows'
and floating voters would appear in the middle. The question
of 'left' and 'right' in this weak sense then reduces to one of the
relationship between political attitudes and voting.

The reader will have noticed the absence in the British poll data
so far cited of any reference to the more bread-and-butter domestic
issues. Here, admittedly, party differences are more notable.
Professor Blondel's researches show differences in 1959–61 on
subjects such as surtax, National Health charges and sympathy
with trade unions or workers on strike. (On nationalisation there
was also a large party gap, with a bare majority of Labour voters
and an overwhelming majority of Conservatives disliking it; but
this is probably by now mainly a symbolic issue.) Yet even on
these domestic topics there was normally much overlapping, with
a large minority of Conservative voters holding 'Labour' views
and vice versa. This is hardly surprising in the light of the fact
that voters in a Bristol survey in 1955 scored only slightly better
than random when asked to identify policy statements with the
party making them.[4]

The connection between party preference and policy views
seems to have become even lower in recent years. An NOP Poll
in 1967 showed not only 77 per cent of Conservative voters
saying that unofficial strikes should be made illegal, but also 68
per cent of Labour voters agreeing with that opinion. Even on the
issue of a means test for the social services there was very little
difference between supporters of the two parties, and there was
only a slight difference on the choice between income tax and taxes
on goods. Asked whether the Government should continue with its

policy of wage restraint, many more Labour than Conservative voters answered 'Yes.' Nobody would, I hope, seriously argue that ideological attitudes to a free market were overriding class interests. It is much more likely that the question was interpreted as a vote of confidence in the Labour Government. The tendency for any question mentioning the word Government, or referring to official policy, to be treated as a straight Labour–Conservative choice is a besetting difficulty in interpreting poll data.

Those issues which did clearly differentiate between Labour and Conservative in the most recent years were in the expected areas, but they take some finding, and the differences between the parties were always moderate. Rather more Labour than Conservative supporters thought that the trade union leaders would be able to keep down wage claims if given a chance. There was more Labour than Conservative support for comprehensive schools. More Labour voters supported defence cuts and more Conservative voters Health Service reductions. (Even so more Conservative voters put defence cuts on their lists of suggested economies than Health Service cuts.) Perhaps most revealing of all was that nearly half of all Conservative supporters agreed that unskilled manual workers were 'getting too much money for the amount of work they do'—an opinion held by only a fifth of Labour supporters. This illustrates the fact that basic party allegiances are accounted for much more by general class impressions than by specific issues. Labour still benefits enormously from its name. Its supporters regard it as the working-class party, in contrast to the Conservatives who are regarded as the party of the rich and big business. The Conservative image among the party's supporters is more diffuse. The concept of a national party, general competence and free enterprise slogans, influence different supporters to different degrees; but a negative reaction to the working-class image of Labour is an important part of the mixture.

These images are partly a reflection of, and partly a cause of, the strongly class-bound pattern of voting, which according to recent studies is more pronounced in Britain than for example in the USA, Canada or Australia.[5] The patterns can be summarised by saying that the middle and upper classes vote overwhelmingly Conservative, while nearly all Labour's support comes from the manual working class. The difference in the way of putting it for the two parties shows how it is possible for there ever to be a

Conservative majority. Manual workers, pensioners and the other categories normally classified as c_2, D or E make up two-thirds of the population and supply about four-fifths of Labour's votes. But a large minority in this group, ranging from about a quarter to a third, support the Conservatives (and slightly under a tenth the Liberals). Such working-class supporters normally make up about half the total Conservative vote. The Party's other main source of support is the lower middle class—the clerical, supervisory and other grades classified as c_1, three-fifths of whom normally vote Conservative. The A and B classes, although they give three-quarters of their votes to the Tories and less than a sixth to Labour, make up only 12 per cent of the population.[6]

In view of the class images of the British parties, the existence of the working-class Conservative has often been regarded as the key puzzle of British politics, and has probably given rise to more nonsense than almost any other political subject. The much-discussed 'deferential' voters in fact account only for a minority of working-class Tories.[7] The most important single explanation probably relates to trade union membership. The expected predominance of Labour voters is indeed found among trade-unionists, but the half or more of the manual workers who are not unionised distribute their votes 'almost at random.'[8] A minority of working-class Conservatives are people who have come to the conclusion that despite Labour's class appeal, the Conservatives will do more for their material prosperity. These are the smiling families pictured around their consumer durables in the posters of the Macmillan era. But the sheer haphazard element in the working-class Tory vote should not be overlooked. We are dealing with the least politically informed section of the population, where sheer inability to pick up the class clues—as distinct from conscious rejection of them—can easily occur. It is because of this innate precariousness of their clientèle that left-wing parties throughout history have always had to hammer home the theme of group loyalty[9]—a good instance being Mr Wilson's habit in his first couple of years of office of referring to 'your Government.'

The pattern of class support for the parties has a close bearing on the very limited policy differences that exist between Labour and Conservative supporters. Left-wing voters believe in a more equal sharing of the national cake and sympathise more than the rest of the electorate with manual workers organised in trade unions. They are not on the whole conscious of potential conflict between these two aims. Right-wing voters are opposed to, or at least do not share, either of them. The critieria for determining whether someone is on the right or on the left in this sense are thus almost exclusively class-related issues. Not only does external policy hardly enter the picture; but even in domestic economic and social policy, the relevant range of issues is very narrow. Economic policy in the sense of growth, full employment and the balance of payments and similar issues about which politicians argue incessantly, are almost as irrelevant. (Voters will have views, varying from time to time, about which party or which leader appears to be more competent at handling these problems; but that is a very different matter from having a specifically left-wing or right-wing view on how they should be handled.) Even opinions on the wider issues of Government intervention versus private enterprise, where they exist at all, are only very marginally related to voting behaviour. Such preferences seem to be linked mainly to those issues where one class gains, or thinks it gains, relative to another.

Left-wing voters do not have any abstract general beliefs about the distribution of income and property. Egalitarianism for them is a matter of vague anti-rich class feelings plus an interest in specific benefits (real or supposed) such as council houses, rent controls, pensions, or a 'free' Health Service. The popular version of the 1959 Labour election manifesto actually had a thumb-index to such benefits with entries such as 'Your House,' 'Your Job,' 'Health,' etc. The Conservatives have the more delicate task of giving the right hints to their middle-class supporters of benefits to come, while being careful to preserve a national appeal so as not to frighten away any of their working-class support.

Of course, expectations may be disappointed, not merely by national economic difficulties which reduce the benefits available for distribution to all classes, but also by the phenomenon of 'leaning over backwards.' A Conservative Government may be so anxious to earn working-class goodwill, and take so much for granted the support of the middle class, that it may actually treat the latter worse than a Labour Government would have done in its place. But such perversity of behaviour has never been persistent enough, or at least obvious enough, to threaten class identification—although there the seeds of such a development have been sown by Labour's incomes policies. If class identifications were ever to be undermined in earnest, there would be no remaining criteria for identifying left and right in the mass electorate.

A curious phenomenon, worth a short digression, is the widespread existence of a sort of moral inferiority complex among many of the more articulate Conservative voters. This has its roots in a tacit acceptance of the claims of socialist egalitarianism to superior virtue over selfish capitalism. Manifestations of this inferiority complex turn up more frequently in conversation than in public utterances. Most people will have heard innumerable remarks, especially by businessmen, that socialism is better in theory, but capitalism is better in practice. The belief is expressed not only in relation to British Labour Governments but sometimes even in connection with Soviet Communism. There are innumerable versions of it, a frequent instance being 'Socialism would be best in an ideal world, but people are not up to it.' A variant common among working-class Conservatives is that Labour politicians are insincere or incompetent. Typical remarks are 'Most of them are after a good job' or 'They like to hear themselves talk.'[10] The expression of positive liberal or conservative beliefs in opposition to Labour's egalitarian appeal is extremely rare outside the political or academic elite. The opposition of thinkers such as Hayek to socialism as a false ideal is not widely echoed, even in the most unacademic form, among the mass of either middle-class or working-class Tories.

It is, however, time to turn from voters to the smaller group of people actively concerned with public affairs. For, if we want to examine the 'strong' concept of a spectrum running from extreme right to extreme left, attention must be focused here. It is only here that we can hope to find sufficient relationship between beliefs on different subjects to make the concept remotely plausible.

To do this it is necessary to examine left and right within each of the two main parties separately, and then see if the two spectra can be joined, with or without an overlap in the middle. This preliminary bisection is unavoidable because the only people to whom varying degrees of left- and right-wing attitudes are publicly ascribed, and on whom data exist, are politicians and party activists. It is easiest to approach the spectrum within each Party by starting from the far ends, the Labour Left and the Tory Right.

This is partly because the users of the left-right spectrum expect to find the most distinctive *doctrines* in these directions. After all, those who regard themselves as on the Tory left or Labour right like to boast that they are not doctrinaire. An additional reason for this procedure is that the more moderate politicians tend to be given their ranking in the scale in relation to their supposed distance from the ends of the spectrum. In what follows where no ambiguity arises, the expressions Left and Right are sometimes used as shorthand for Labour Left and Conservative Right.

Even at these two extremes, politicians are not expected to subscribe to unified belief systems, such as Marxism in its heyday, covering every political issue. There are no beliefs common to all members of either extreme. The Labour Left and the Tory Right are cluster concepts. The holding of a selection among a set of characteristic beliefs qualifies a person for membership; but within the cluster there will be people whose beliefs do not overlap at all. There are very few individual beliefs which are in themselves sufficient to earn a Left or Right label, although, this generalisation is more true of the Conservative than of the Labour Party. For there are one or two attitudes, such as an active belief in Clause 4, which are probably in themselves sufficient for membership of the Labour Left, if not in the eyes of other Left-wingers, at least in the eyes of the rest of the Party.

One of the very few published studies of the links between MPs' views on different subjects is the work by Finer, Berrington and Bartholomew on Early Day Motions, in the 1955–9 Parliament.[11] Few, if any, of these Motions are actually debated, but they are not subject to the control of the Whips and provide a good opportunity for the expression of back-bench views. The Motions analysed covered a great variety of subjects, from the cost of living and social security to German rearmament and the H-bomb. Not surprisingly, a Labour MP who signed one Motion was somewhat more likely to have signed another Motion than a colleague who did not. Much more interesting was the pattern of correlation between the different types of Motions signed by Labour Members. These were relatively high correlations between the degree of support for unilateral nuclear disarmament, the degree of support for European disengagement and the recognition of East Germany. The association was nearly as strong between heretical Motions on foreign policy and the number of 'anti-colonialist' Motions signed. There was some, although slightly smaller, connection between these 'left-wing' attitudes on foreign policy and the tendency to sign Motions calling for a more humanitarian penal approach, or drawing attention to infringements of civil liberty.

There was also a significant degree of overlapping among those who signed Motions attacking the Conservative Government for the high cost of living, for interfering with Arbitration Tribunals, for not spending enough on health and education, and calling for an increase in social security benefits. But the correlation between signature of these materialist motions and either foreign policy dissent or humanitarian zeal was small and sometimes negligible. The materialist Motions were on the whole somewhat unsophisticated demands and protests in keeping with the working-class image of the Labour movement. They were in no meaningful sense left-wing in Labour Party terms. The cluster of MPs who tended to sign the heretical Motions on foreign policy and defence, and also displayed some zeal for humanitarian reform, constituted the Left of the Party in the simple sense that they were regarded as such both by themselves and the outside world.

The Early Day Motions of the 1955–9 Parliament did not show what the Left thought on economic and social questions. This was not a coincidence; for the main interest of this group of MPs was then in foreign affairs and remained so until the freeze and squeeze of 1966. Nevertheless, as a matter of linguistic usage, any MP who was a Socialist in the Clause 4 sense of the term, and paid more than lip service to 'common ownership,' would have been classified as on the Left. In addition the Left was (and still is) characterised by a devotion to the principle of universal and free welfare benefits. Whether this was because of any logical relation to its other beliefs, or due to the historical accident that Bevan had been its leader, is debatable. On the other hand, as Alan Watkins has remarked, the Bevanites had never been particularly interested in economic egalitarianism, in fact less so than the Gaitskellite revisionists.[12]

In the 1950s it was still just possible to define a spectrum in the Parliamentary Labour Party in terms of distance from the Left. Even then the notion was a considerable oversimplification. It was quite impossible to say whether the 'revisionist' intellectuals, such as Crosland and Jenkins, were to the left or the right of the solid loyalist MPs who were at least verbally committed to the Party's traditional anti-capitalist attitude but who on most non-class matters were no more radical than the Tory knights of the shires. In the 1960s, and especially since the return of Labour to power in 1964, the spectrum concept became increasingly difficult to apply to Labour MPs. On a growing number of issues one could argue endlessly about which attitudes should be labelled left, right or centre—which is the death-blow to any spectrum theory. In the pre-devaluation period, some of the strongest criticisms of the Government's deflationary economic policies came from MPs (and Ministers) who were regarded as Gaitskellite right-wingers. Attitudes to the Common Market also cut across the Party's traditional left–right division. Even on Vietnam, signatures of Motions critical of US policy ranged well outside the normal group of Left-wingers.

It is not merely the issues that have become more difficult to classify in left–right terms, but the Labour MPs themselves. A large number of the newer Members are, as a recent study puts it, 'increasingly difficult to type-cast as being left, right or centre.' This stems partly from the increasing proportion of professional and middle-class Labour MPs who lack the trade union traditions of solidarity. 'As free-wheeling individualists, their policy positions are somewhat unpredictable'; they may well support the Leadership on some issues and oppose it on others.[13]

Although the plausibility of a continuous left–right scale along which Labour MPs can be graded has disappeared, the hard-core Left is still very much alive as a political entity. It is, I think, fair to say that common to most of the Left is a fundamentalist hostility to the rules of the game of a mixed capitalist economy. This was for a long time overlaid by the concentration on foreign policy, but came to the surface again in the Left's opposition to the measures required to make devaluation work. The attitudes involved include a deep suspicion of Keynesian economic management (often allied with a failure to comprehend it); an unwillingness to accept the role of profits, which is naturally coupled with a desire to control prices but not wages; a tendency to blame Britain's troubles on foreign bankers; and an advocacy of the devices of a siege economy. MPs outside the Left frequently voice some of these sentiments, which sometimes colour even Ministerial pronouncements, although less often affect their actual behaviour. Indeed few Labour Members, outside the ranks of those who happen to be economists or have had business experience, accept the morality of the profit motive and the market economy in the way that most European Social Democrats now do. (Harold Wilson himself is extremely ambivalent on these points.) The difference is that the loyalists are prepared to accept as a practical necessity policies which they would never take from a Conservative Government.

The Left is characterised by a greater mistrust of the official leadership, and a greater tendency to carry its views to the Division Lobby, than the rest of the Parliamentary Party. This probably explains why it made the running in the fight against wage restraint and curbs on the growth of social expenditure, which the rest of the Party was prepared to accept, however reluctantly, when the Government was labelled 'Labour.' Indeed, for many purposes the hard-core Left is best regarded as a group of nameable individuals. These were originally defined in terms of foreign policy and personal support of Aneurin Bevan, but being on the Left is becoming more and more a matter of group identification. Members of the Left have a special loyalty to each other; the expression 'party within a party' is fundamentally correct. A Motion is identified as left-wing by the names on it as well as by the content.

One problem is that of the relationship of the Labour Left to the extreme left in the shape of Soviet or Chinese-type Communism. Now one of the sufficient (although not necessary) conditions for counting a Labour MP as a member of the Left was for a long time a certain sympathy for Communist countries —especially for their views in international disputes. It is therefore tempting to see a continuum extending from the Labour Left to the Communists. But it would be misleading to do so. For the qualities that characterised the international Communist movement in its heyday were a rigid discipline, a readiness to use force and a general intolerance of dissent. The Labour Left, on the other hand, has usually had a dislike of force in international affairs and an intense distaste for Party (or any other) discipline. Some of the hawk-like qualities exhibited by the Communists were in fact closer to those of the extreme right than the Labour Left. This is another area where a simple left–right measuring-rod failed to work.

The remarks are put into the past tense, because readiness to co-operate with the Soviet Union, and sympathise with its view-point, are no longer an exclusively Left attribute. Indeed, with Russia becoming an increasingly conservative world power, the sympathies of the Labour Left are directed more towards Africa and the undeveloped world. Opposition to the Vietnam War was, after 1964, a point of contact between past and present attitudes. But such opposition, although perhaps a necessary condition, was not a sufficient condition for being on the Left. It was shared by people whose attitudes on other questions disqualified them for being counted as on the left in the Labour versus Conservative sense, let alone as on the Left of the Labour Party. In the USA some of the leading opponents of the official Vietnam policy included men such as Senator Fulbright and G. F. Kennan, who on many other subjects would be regarded as fairly conservative.

If the notion of a left–right spectrum has become difficult to apply to the Parliamentary Labour Party, it is almost impossible to apply to Conservative MPs. Professor Finer's investigations failed to distinguish many significant correlations between the views of Conservative MPs on different types of subjects. A Member who held 'right-wing' views on one issue was as likely as not to hold 'left-wing' views on other issues. Instead of perman-ent groups, there were constant realignments as new issues came to the fore and the opponents of one day became the allies of another. (To this extent the Conservatives in Parliament resemble the electorate at large.)

There were, however, local correlations. There was some overlap between those who were pro-Empire and anti-European, the Suez die-hards and the signatories of anti-UN Motions. Nearly half of the relatively small group of declared Suez die-hards signed pro-Empire Motions which were also anti-European. Again, nearly half the die-hards signed anti-UN Motions. Thus there was a nucleus of a 'foreign policy Right,' although it was small in number and covered a much smaller range of questions than the Labour Left. There was, moreover, no association between views on foreign affairs and views on social and economic policy.

There was a modest correlation between 'left-wing' attitudes to social policy (such as deploring the British Motor Corporation's action in 1956 in dismissing workers at short notice, or calling for the wider distribution of individual property) and concern for civil liberties. The one correlation between home and foreign policy was that nearly half the Suez die-hards—fifteen Members— had 'severe' attitudes to penal reform. There was, however, no such tendency among those who were 'moderately right-wing' on Suez in the sense of strongly supporting Eden's action and voicing fierce resentment of American attitudes. But even in the case of the strongest connections, the degree of overlap was much less than existed on the Labour side between the different components of the Left-wing syndrome. Moreover on several key issues, such as crime and punishment, and Empire versus Europe, the difference was mainly one of generation rather than of left and right.

While Labour has been a party of factions, the Conservatives have, at least in Parliament, been a party of tendencies.[14] There is a wealth of evidence that Conservative M Ps judge their leaders far more in terms of ability and success, than in ideological terms. It was remarkable what an extraordinarily small part policy issues played in the choice between Heath and Maudling, or even in the agonised debate on the merits of Sir Alec Douglas-Home as Leader. Such an approach to politics has its drawbacks. While policy statements and speeches are perhaps taken over-seriously by Labour Members, Conservatives tend to underrate them, regarding them as a sort of 'prep' which may be well or badly done rather than as subjects over which adults disagree. (One of the besetting temptations in writing about the Conservative Party is to over-use public-school metaphors.) There is, moreover an inarticulate quality about a great deal of Conservative thinking, both on issues and personalities. As much importance is attached to what is not said as to what is; and some cryptic indications of a change of attitude from two or three senior bell-wether figures are worth many hours or pages of verbalised argument.

Having said all this, it is not so easy to dismiss the concept of a Conservative Right. Professor Finer's researches show some signs, in the early years of the 1959–64 Parliament, of a stronger overlap between support for the reintroduction of judicial corporal punishment and disquiet at the pace of African enfranchisement in Northern Rhodesia than existed between such subjects in the previous Parliament.[15] It is possible that this trend has continued. This is not, however, the crucial consideration. For whether it is significantly represented in the House of Commons or not, a Tory

Right most certainly does exist, for example among constituency parties and among Conservative activists up and down the country. It is difficult to depict its attitudes without being guilty of caricature. Nevertheless a selection from among the following would be sufficient to merit the description Right-winger in normal political usage: sympathy for the Ian Smith regime in Rhodesia; support for hanging and flogging; strong hostility to the 'permissive' society; belief that British troops should have been sent to Vietnam; advocacy of a larger margin of unemployment and a hard line on immigration and race relations. Nobody who has ears to hear can deny that extreme support for a generous sample of these attitudes can be found among a large number of the British middle class. These were often joined in the winter of 1967–8 with a belief in some sort of business government to run 'Great Britain Ltd.'

An analogous problem to the relation between the Labour Left and Communism is that between the Conservative Right and Fascism. It is also a more elusive problem. For while Communism can be more or less identified and recognised, there has been no distinguishing badge to mark out a regime as Fascist, a word which is in any case now much more emotive than descriptive. All one can say is that there are several dictatorships in the world which can be described as right-wing because they are based either on enforced obedience to what is regarded as traditional authority, or on militant anti-Communism, or on both. These regimes are of varying degree of oppressiveness. In some ways dictatorships such as Franco's Spain, that of the Greek colonels, or the white oligarchy of South Africa, have a better claim to be regarded as extreme right than Mussolini's Italy or Hitler's Germany. For the latter incorporated in their appeal many elements of populist anti-upper-class feeling absent from genuine right-wing dictatorships.

At first sight the attitude of the Tory Right to such Governments seems very similar to that of the Labour Left to Communist ones. In both cases the British politicians concerned would indignantly repudiate any sympathy for their repressive internal features, but would tend to find extenuating circumstances and, more important, be concerned to avoid any hostile international treatment of them. Many Tories, not only on the Right, would assert that their party is less inclined to sit in judgment on the internal regimes of other countries than Labour and that therefore the analogy is not a fair one. On the other hand, most of the Labour Left are temperamentally doves, while Communism is by nature a hawk-like movement. There is not quite this temperamental chasm between the Tory Right and right-wing dictatorships, which are both 'hawk' phenomena, although in greatly varying degrees.

Despite the lack of correlation between the views of Conservative Members on different policy matters, the Press does talk of a Conservative Left; and it is worth asking to what the label refers. At the time of writing there seem to be at least three Conservative lefts. There is the Maudling left, characterised by a belief in incomes policy and a reluctance to throw over indicative planning, the Boyle–Chataway school which has some sympathy for comprehensive schools, and an anti-racialist left consisting either of those who supported the Labour Government's Rhodesian policy (and may even have wanted it to have gone further), or of those who were anxious to prevent the Tory line on immigration from becoming too hard.

It is most unlikely that there is much interrelation between these groups. Mr Terence Higgins, who voted for oil sanctions against Rhodesia but has a full-blooded market approach to economic questions, is a good illustration. Probably the main point of contact between at least two out of three Tory lefts is Sir Edward Boyle, who in addition to his educational views, is a supporter of incomes policy and indicative planning. Quite apart from its non-existence as a single group, the interesting feature of the Tory left is the limited range of issues it covers. (Contrary to what is often supposed, incomes policy and indicative planning are relatively minor parts of economic policy.)

It was mentioned earlier that more and more issues were arising in the Labour Party, on which it was not even possible to say which were the left-wing and which the right-wing sides. While this is perhaps a comparatively recent phenomenon among Labour, Professor Finer found it well established among issues that interested Conservative M Ps as long ago as the 1950s. He mentions demands for the abolition of Schedule A, and for an easing of the earnings rule for pensioners, as typical unclassifiable examples.

The degree of opposition expressed to economic egalitarianism has almost no relevance to left–right classifications among Conservative politicians. Even the most anti-egalitarian opinions do not put a Conservative anywhere near the right of his Party, if he steers clear of right-wing attitudes on say, crime and Africa. In the week or so before writing this passage, the most outspoken condemnations of egalitarianism have come from Iain Macleod and Christopher Chataway. The most one can say is that some right-wing Conservatives attach more value than Mr Macleod or Mr Chataway, not to economic inequality, but to social status of a hereditary and basically pre-capitalist kind. (So incidentally do some Labour voters, although not Labour politicians.)

If attitudes to economic equality are irrelevant to left–right distinctions among Conservatives, so too are many wider issues of social policy. Some years ago left–right attitudes in the Tory Party were sometimes demarcated, even by academic writers, in terms of the cliché 'acceptance of the Welfare State.' Arguments that more could be done for the most deserving by greater selectivity, by cash grants in place of subsidised houses, or ideas for cashable vouchers to encourage private education, were regarded as very right-wing, a description which was intended to be pejorative. Now that fashions have changed and even many in the Labour Party favour more selectivity this terminology has fortunately dropped out of use, and attitudes to the social services are no longer used to measure a politician's position in the Conservative spectrum. This was always a mistake. Iain Macleod, who infuriated the Tory Right with his African policies and was publicly critical of the closed Etonian circle, was one of the earliest and most forthright opponents of the universal provision of state welfare.

On economic policy there has been a long-standing difference between the paternalist Tory tendency, which has included Disraeli, Joseph Chamberlain and Macmillan, and the free-market liberals, now most vociferously represented by Enoch Powell. (It is interesting that none of the prominent leaders of the Conservative Party in the past was an unequivocal liberal.) There is no meaningful sense in which one tendency can be said to be to the left or the right of the other. Devotion to the market economy can certainly not be identified with the Tory Right. Indeed, it is among the latter group that protectionist sentiment has always been strongest. In the last Conservative Government the most self-consciously upper-class Ministers were the least worried about the suppression of the market mechanism; nor is it entirely a coincidence that enthusiasm for the market mechanism is to be found more among Redbrick than among Oxbridge economists.

Indeed, the more one looks into it, the more one is struck by the irrelevance of most economic and social issues to a person's place in any attempted Conservative spectrum. The existence of the Maudlingite left is a partial exception to this general rule in one limited field. If a Conservative MP is pro-flogging and hanging, wishes we had never left Egypt, would like British troops to fight in Vietnam and would put Mrs Whitehouse in charge of all television, it would not make an iota of difference to his Right-wing classification whether he supported Maudling or Powell on incomes policy. If an MP with the other general attitudes stated were also highly paternalist and believed in large welfare benefits for all, it would still not detract from his Right-wing status. As for the supposed argument between state intervention and the market economy, it hardly enters the picture at all. Our hypothetical Right-wing Conservative might be anything from a strong opponent of commercial values, who believed in legislation against advertising, 'buying British,' and statutory controls over wages and prices, to a fervent exponent of the free play of market forces. It is difficult to say which would enhance his Right-wing status more.

Some writers would identify the Right, not with the economic liberal, but with the interests of Big Business as such, irrespective of doctrine. This, however, is most implausible. The previous chapter has shown how limited in time and extent the association between capitalism and the Tory Right has been even in the past; and in recent years it has been even smaller. The issues which are exciting the Tory Right at the time of writing are Rhodesia, immigration and the British withdrawal from East of Suez. The Right-wing troubles in the 1959–64 Parliament were on African advancement, judicial corporal punishment, the European Economic Community, and the credibility of the nuclear deterrent after the cancellation of Skybolt. These were anything but Big Business interests. The anti-EEC group was in fact opposed to the main Big Business and City lobbies. The resale price maintenance revolt was essentially a small business affair—although it is doubtful

whether it should be labelled 'Right-wing.' The only major Big
Business interest identified with the Tory Right was the aerospace
lobby; it is hardly a coincidence that this is the one industry
where the commercial interests overlap with military ones and feed
on the emotions of those who regret the passing of Britain's Great
Power role.

If we glance abroad, the lack of any special correlation between
capitalism and the extreme right wing is even more apparent.
The regime of the Colonels which gained control in Greece in 1967
almost immediately took a large number of *dirigiste* measures. It
was made an offence, punishable by imprisonment, for any Greek
citizen to earn more than the Prime Minister, and a committee
was appointed to draft a Five-Year Plan.[16] In Koestler's *Darkness
at Noon*, the counter-revolutionary in the neighbouring cell to the
hero's is not a capitalist, but a Cossack officer. Schumpeter made
some profound observations on the incapacity of the capitalist
bourgeoisie for politics,[17] which is amply confirmed by observations
of the Confederation of British Industry in Britain. In Thomas
Mann's *The Magic Mountain*, the formidable right-wing opponent
of the visionary liberal Settembrini is a Socialist Jesuit priest who
glories in the impending doom of capitalism. To take a more
topical example, Governor Reagan, like other presidential aspir-
ants of the right before him, was backed by small rather than big
business. As Governor of California his targets were not the
'workers' or the lower-paid but the weak and the unpopular—
'Negroes, the mentally ill, the university, beatniks and drugs.'[18]

If nothing else, this chapter should have convinced the reader
that the rules for applying the concepts left and right are complicated, ill-defined and often ambiguous. I regret if this confusion
has been too faithfully reflected in my own exposition. How, at the
end of it all, is one to assess the utility of the left–right scale? It
will help if we keep in mind that the main test of any political
classification is its ability to identify long-lasting dispositions from
which attitudes to individual issues can be predicted. Moderately
successful predictions of this kind might be made about politicians
on the Labour Left and—with much greater difficulty—on the
Tory Right. But the left–right spectrum is far less likely to be
successful for those anywhere between these extremes. For the
lack of correlation between attitudes to different questions among

such people makes prediction extremely hazardous. A new 'slightly right-of-centre' Minister, of either party, could earn this label by any number of utterly different policy mixtures. A second and even greater difficulty is added by the large and growing number of subjects where it is impossible even to say what is a right-wing and what is a left-wing policy. A third source of trouble is the instability of labels which are given to particular viewpoints. What may count as an extreme right-wing opinion at one time may, only a little while later, be regarded as not particularly right-wing at all, as in the case of 'selectivity.'

Even if these difficulties could be overcome, there is the further complication that the issues which are used for classifying left and right in the two main parties are different, so that the two halves of the spectrum cannot be joined to give a continuous scale. The relevant issues in the Labour Party cover, *inter alia*, attitudes to 'free' social welfare benefits, the degree of acceptance of private enterprise and the profit motive, and the extent of support for Western Cold War positions. Among Conservatives they include the degree of attachment to Britain's world role, attitudes to Africa and immigration, and positions on crime and punishment. Moreover the class-related issues which are most relevant to the choice between left and right among the electorate have hardly any bearing at all on how far to the right or left a politician is reckoned to be inside his own party.

A number of interesting political attitudes not only cannot be placed on a spectrum, but cannot even be classified as left or right in the weaker Labour–Conservative sense. Hostility to profit maximisation and to commercial values can be equally regarded as a fundamentalist Socialist attitude, or as typical of a certain brand of Tory traditionalism. With a certain type of anti-com-commercial, anti-urban writing, it is quite impossible to tell whether the author is a member of the New Left or the Old Right. A great many passages in the works of E. J. Mishan, the anti-growth economist, could equally fit either standpoint.[19] A dislike of the attempted 'special relationship' with the USA may be equally characteristic of the Labour Left, the Tory Right or some of the 'Europeans' in the middle.

Moreover, in concentrating on practising politicians, the above discussion has intentionally been biased in favour of the left–right spectrum. For the main party alignments are systematically biased to reduce the representation in the House of certain combinations of opinions. A pacifist who proclaimed the virtues of the capitalist system would find no place in the British House of Commons; those who combine a dove-like approach to foreign affairs with a free-enterprise bias at home are seriously under-represented. A high correlation between approval of American Far Eastern policies and opposition to price control in the UK may simply indicate that Conservative associations tend to select as candidates people who combine these two attitudes. It may not imply any correlation between the two attitudes among informed opinion in the country at large, still less a logical correlation between them.

So much for the weaknesses of left and right as a universal system of political classification. The next chapter turns to the more important task of demonstrating that the system is also harmful.

4 / THE HARM
THAT IS DONE

It is the character of the British people, or at least of the higher and middle classes who pass muster for the British people, that to induce them to approve of any change, it is necessary that they should look upon it as a middle course; they think every proposal extreme and violent unless they hear of some other proposal going still further upon which their antipathy to extreme views may discharge itself.

J. S. MILL, *Autobiography*

We HAVE SEEN FROM THE PREVIOUS CHAPTER that it is possible to make sense of the left–right classification if it is used in a weak sense in relation to people's attitudes to the two main parties. If being on the left is *defined* as having a greater propensity to vote Labour than Conservative, and vice versa, then a simple model can be constructed. Left and right then turn largely on class. The right-wing party is the one that receives the overwhelming majority of middle- and upper-class votes. Left-wing support is almost entirely concentrated in the working class, although there is of course a large minority of working-class Tories—without whom there would never be a Conservative Government.

This sociological pattern is confirmed by views on issues. Voters in each camp are unified by views on a very narrow range of class matters. Left-wing voters favour measures which they think will put money into the hands of the lower-paid, while right-wing voters are concerned to gain more for the middle class and are also more hostile to trade unions. But there is little tendency for Labour and Conservative voters to have distinctive partisan views on other issues. Limited in this way, left and right would describe a narrow closed circle relating to class membership, feelings towards different social groups and to the trade unions, attitudes to economic egalitarianism, and voting propensities: a closed, banal, and boring system, but the whole of domestic politics for those without imagination.

Even this weak sense of left and right does some harm. The reformer who wants to make radical fiscal changes, both to provide more incentives and to make a more fundamental attack on the present maldistribution of wealth, while eliminating the hypocrisy and absurdity of nominally high tax rates, is classified in exactly the same way as the man who wants no change, or who wants to split the difference between the front benches. This is if he is fortunate enough to have his views assessed by skilled political researchers. He is more likely to be regarded as an untrustworthy red agitator on the right, and as a capitalist stooge on the left. This is no more than to say that a straight-line classification best suits those who think in stereotyped terms, and has no way of separating constructive ideas from conventional middle-of-the-road compromises.

The left–right classification is, however, open to much stronger objection when it comes to non-class issues, where views, certainly among the public but also among politicians, cut across party lines. Whenever such issues are more important than cake-dividing squabbles, the real division between people is not adequately represented by the Conservative–Labour battle, and still less by the stronger idea of a continuous spectrum stretching from the Labour Left to the Tory Right.

The survival of an inappropriate terminology cannot be dismissed as a mere commentator's mistake. For it affects the conduct as well as the description of politics. Language influences actions; the myth of the left–right spectrum influences the policies that people are prepared to champion and the associates with whom they are prepared to work. The spectrum concept isolates a Labour Left and a Conservative Right, but wrongly assumes that there is a continuous line running between them. It uses the popular dislike of the extremes to convey an aura of reasonableness to policies on which the two front benches agree; and any critic of such policies can be smeared by politicians who seize on any overlap between his views and those of the right or left extremes.

Numerous examples of the ambiguity or non-applicability of the left–right measuring rod have been given in preceding chapters. It has been shown that it is impossible to place differing Tory economic views on a left–right scale. An equally strong case can be made for putting the economic liberals to the left or to the right of the interventionists. In both parties, and among opinion generally, left and right were irrelevant to the most important issues of the middle 1960s—devaluation and the Common Market.

Ronald Butt concludes his study of Parliament by remarking that the present malaise has nothing to do with its processes and procedures but stems from the fact that 'the real arguments of politics have increasingly come to lie across Party lines,'[1] and *a fortiori* across left–right distinctions. Devaluation, which was the major talking-point of the middle 1960s, was, he remarks, 'virtually taken out of politics by mutual consent.'[2] Although the Common Market looked on a couple of occasions like becoming a major issue between the parties, it never did; the most important aspects of the argument, such as the conflict between Britain's European aspirations and the idea of a special relationship with the Americans, or the question of alternatives such as either a North Atlantic Free Trade Area or economic association with the EEC, never got anywhere near the surface of political debate. After the 1967 devaluation there was a considerable consensus about what had to be done to make devaluation work among those who understood the subject; but it was expressed in terms of regulating demand and freeing resources, which had no meaning to those who thought in terms of left and right. One could go on indefinitely listing the major issues of foreign, defence and economic policy—and even many issues in education, health and penal matters—which are the real subjects of behind-the-scenes and specialised argument, but are quite outside the left–right debate.

A similar and justified feeling that the party political debate was sterile and irrelevant to the real issues was evident in the 1930s, when Churchill proposed an economic sub-Parliament. The few people who then saw what needed to be done—a strangely assorted group including Keynes, Lloyd George, Mosley and to some extent the young Harold Macmillan—did not form a coherent group in the left–right spectrum at all. One could say that they were in the centre in that they wanted neither to abandon capitalism nor to retreat into *immobilisme*, but to make capitalism work by increasing purchasing power. But this only shows the dangerous ambiguity of the whole centre concept. The açcolade of centre was more frequently bestowed on the MacDonald–Baldwin coalition, whose response to slump and unemployment was to accept the respectable advice to reduce spending further. In fact the cleavage between the economic radicals and conservatives, both in the 1930s and in the period before the 1967 devaluation, cut completely across the capitalist–socialist and egalitarian–elitist arguments.

It would be unrealistic to put all the blame on the left–right concept as such. The present nature of the party system, to be discussed in Chapter 6, has much to answer for. In addition the technical nature of so many contemporary issues—both when the experts disagree and when there is a consensus—would in any case make it very difficult to make the political argument turn on them. It would be hard to return to the nineteenth-century situation when the party battle reflected a few simple issues such as free trade, Home Rule or Parliamentary reform, in the light of which the parties broke up and regrouped. Yet the left–right approach does aggravate matters by putting all the stress on those few topics, relating mostly to the working-class–middle-class tensions, which can still be put in these terms. It causes unnecessary public confusion over the real nature of our problems, and encourages both spectators and participants to take the Labour–Conservative argument with excessive seriousness, instead of as a convenient way of running a competitive political system.

There is a deeper way in which the attempt to apply an outmoded left–right scale to the whole range of political issues does harm. Consider the case of someone whose sympathies are more with private enterprise and the profit motive than with state economic intervention, and who rejects at least the cruder versions of Labour egalitarianism. Thus on the key issues which determine party allegiance—the first in theory and the second in both theory and practice—he would be classified as on the right. Let us suppose he is also a liberal and radical on many issues; that he is in sympathy with Mill's concept of personal liberty (lately rechristened by its opponents as the 'permissive society'); that he wanted to abandon Britain's world-policeman role long before this view became fashionable, that he was nauseated by British support of the Vietnam War and that he is fond of talking about the Foreign Office's remarkable record of misconceived advice. Even on economic policy he may think that the real mistake was to hang on to the $2.80 parity for too long, and he may favour reducing the international financial role of sterling as fast as is practicable.

Such a person will certainly be distrusted in Conservative circles as a far-out left-winger, much more dangerous than the average Labour voter or solid trade union M Ps (who are really 'good chaps'). In addition to his deserved notoriety because of his various heresies, it will also be assumed quite falsely on the right that he has 'socialist' economic views, and this assumption will cloud the reception of what he has to say. On the other hand, if he is at all honest about his views on profits and egalitarianism, he will be bitterly scorned in genuinely left-wing circles. There will thus be an enormous temptation to play down his less congenial views to receive a better reception in one camp or the other.

Someone who does not hold strong views on class-related matters or egalitarianism, and believes that the really important issues are in other areas, should not attempt to place himself on the left–right spectrum at all. The spectrum works by a policy of exclusion. Where a person has a mixture of views, left-wingers will look at the ones that shock them most and conclude that he is an incorrigible right-winger, and vice versa. Those who are tempted to say 'Hard luck,' should pause to ask whether the left–right dialogue has really been so fruitful over the last twenty years that other groupings of ideas should be excluded from consideration.

The harm done by the spectrum theory can be summarised under two headings: the revulsion from the extremes, and the rush towards the 'centre.' From the very way in which the spectrum is defined—with Clause 4, beards and guitars at one end, and white supremacy and birching at the other—the term 'centre' becomes one of commendation.

The 'centre' is usually defined in relation to the middle ground (or area of overlap) between Labour and Conservative policies. Anyone who disagrees with this prevailing consensus can be written off as an extremist by definition. The same blessed epithet of centre was applied to those policies of a Labour Government —such as the creation of unemployment in 1966 or the support of the more doubtful aspects of U S foreign policy—which caused the greatest fury among Labour supporters. It is also applied to those policies of the 1951–64 Conservative Governments—such as maintaining unrealistically high surtax rates, or appeasement of the unions—which won applause from the other side of the House and which made Conservative supporters feel uneasy.

Just as the spectrum concept puts dissenters at a disadvantage, so it puts certain official policies at an unmerited advantage. Because the extreme left was disliked for good reasons, and because Mr Wilson ostentatiously turned against it in his early years of office, many writers thought he deserved praise, and in particular for the policies which most antagonised the left. The fallacy here is that the grounds on which the Prime Minister antagonised the left may have had very little to do with those aspects of the left-wing cluster of ideas that are deservedly unpopular.

One reason for treating the centre with less than the customary respect is that it so often tends to follow rather than lead opinion. Its advocates tend to shift enormously, but with a time-lag, under the influence of more positive viewpoints, and today's centre is often yesterday's extreme. Not long ago reform of trade union legislation was regarded as an extreme right-wing proposition. So was any idea of encroachment upon the principle of universal benefits. Today, thanks partly to the efforts of their sponsors, these ideas are regarded as only just (if at all) right of centre. Examples of extreme left ideas which have been taken over by the centre include the withdrawal from the East-of-Suez role and the treatment of the USSR not as an outright enemy, but as a country with certain shared interests in containing conflict. The 'centre' can thus easily seem a soggy ground, occupied by people who respond belatedly to the ideas of others and who will always bow towards the prevailing wind.

Almost as much harm is done by the automatic and unreasoned revulsion from the extremes as by sanctification of the centre. The Labour Left and Tory Right are associated with a number of ideas which many people, for very good reasons, find abhorrent. From this they draw the false inference that they must never be found in the company of either of these extremes. The negative power of the two extremes has varied in different periods. At the time of writing the main bogey is the Labour Left; and virtually all Conservative politicians, and many Labour ones too, would want at all costs to avoid seeming to share any of its thinking; and the same applies to the whole mass of middle-of-the-road commentators, institutes concerned with current affairs, and opinion-formers generally.

Most unconventional ideas, however, will seem initially far removed from the 'centre,' both because they will be nowhere near the range of cross-bench consensus, and because they are likely to have some supporters among the Labour Left, the Tory Right, or both. Thus they are doubly smeared, even though there is nothing in the heretical ideas in any way related to the dislikable features of either the extreme right or the extreme left. Because the

Labour Left is wrong on Clause 4, or selective in the countries against which it will protest, it does not follow that Britain should have supported the USA in Vietnam. Because the Left is unreasonable in its demands for universal welfare benefits, it does not follow that it is wrong on European disengagement. Because the attitudes of the Tory Right to Africa, or crime and punishment, are distasteful, it does not follow that the demand by some of its members for a joint European defence system is wrong. Nor does it mean that the dislike felt in sections of both the Tory Right and the Labour Left of Britain's excessive tendency to toe the American line should be pushed aside. Yet this is the kind of nonsense argument to which people are driven by looking at what the extreme left and extreme right are advocating, and then saying the opposite.

The result is that dissenters against any of the front-bench policies of the moment are too easily written off as extremist, far removed from the middle ground for which the two parties are supposed to be fighting. There is therefore enormous pressure to support the conventionally enlightened policies of the moment with sentiments such as: 'You can't be against incomes policies and put yourself in the same camp as Enoch Powell and Frank Cousins'; or 'How can you be against raising the compulsory school-leaving age—even the more enlightened Tories, such as Sir Edward Boyle, are in favour?'

To take another example, one would have thought anyone of almost any political view would have shrunk back from what was perpetrated in Vietnam in the name of 'deterring Communist aggression.' Did one have to be a Socialist, still less a left-wing one, to have feelings of revulsion when one read about hospitals, filled two or three to a bed with victims of American bombing from villages in the Vietcong areas? The weapons employed included napalm and white phosphorus. The bodies of their victims were drowned in flames, but they tended to 'live' afterwards. Then there was 'Lazy Dog' sending up to 10,000 steel darts through the air which can kill over 800 square yards. 'Beyond that it merely maims, amputating a leg more surely than could a surgeon's knife.' This was all part of a policy of burning the Vietcong off the ground.[3] It was no answer to quote instances of Vietcong atrocities. The whole scale of the conflict (as in Korea previously) was transformed by the American involvement. The whole country and many of its people will have been destroyed, burned or maimed, whether or not it is in the end 'saved from Communism,' whatever that may mean.

Destruction, suffering and oppression may sometimes be a necessary evil to prevent even greater quantities of these same misfortunes. To assess whether this is so in particular cases, the vague abstractions about 'aggression,' 'standing up to Communism,' 'the domino theory' and all the rest need to be translated into statements relating to individual men and women who alone can suffer, die or feel free. No one has shown that the Vietnam War could survive an analysis in these terms; and if there was any uncertainty in this matter—of comparing present murder, torture and oppression with hypothetical deterrent effects—the benefit of the doubt should surely have been given all along to those who wanted the American involvement reduced rather than increased.

There has always been cruelty, horror and sadism in the world— often, as in this case, in the name of high principles and deeper political wisdom—and the British cannot feel moral responsibility for everything that happens. This country's moral involvement arose only because of the policy of giving gratuitous backing to the American side. Yet the Government allowed itself in 1964 to become so dependent on American financial support to save the pound (an endeavour that had the failure it so richly deserved) that its freedom to dissociate from US Vietnam policy could be called into question; and so insensitive had political opinion become that there was no outcry against the state of affairs, least of all from the Conservative 'Opposition.' Both Mr Heath with his policy of 'all the way with L.B.J.' and the Labour Government itself were left high and dry when Lyndon Johnson seemed to change course in the spring of 1968.

One reason why the Wilson Government and the Conservative leadership were allowed to get away with their Vietnam policy was that the attacks on it came from the Labour Left. Yet why should the British middle classes have been committed to support US policy in Vietnam because they disagreed with nationalisation, the sequestration of the overseas portfolio, hostility to profits, high taxation and universal social services? The enormous harm done by the concept of a syndrome of left-wing policies was aptly symbolised by a remark made to me by an up-and-coming representative of progressive Toryism, who said that he instinctively felt that if any view was expressed by 'Michael Foot and his friends' this was a good enough reason for opposing it. This kind of thinking in stereotypes is all too typical of the politically articulate classes. (Sometimes it seems that the ill-informed majority who do not know 'what goes with what' have a better instinct than the supposedly more sophisticated MPs and journalists.) The left–right model puts together in boxes a whole set of logically unconnected ideas, and forces voters to accept or refute them *en bloc*.

One misfortune is that the Labour Left in its present form plays into the hands of the conventional wisdom. If it did not exist, it would have to be invented as a bogey. In many ways it is an anachronism, associating under one umbrella a whole variety of ideas, good and bad, which do not belong together. By insisting on their corporate identity, members do harm to their own most important causes. People may nowadays be drawn to the Labour Left for humanitarian or foreign-policy reasons which have nothing to do with Clause 4, or extreme egalitarianism. Some of them may even feel with Dr Johnson that a man is never more harmlessly employed than in making money. Yet as a result of their inherent beliefs and traditions the Left felt bound to fight for steel nationalisation as hard as against British nuclear weapons, despite the complete irrelevance of steel nationalisation to Britain in the 1960s or 1970s. There was even a time when the Prime Minister hoped to defeat left-wing attitudes on unemployment or foreign policy by some enabling legislation for a marginal extension of state shareholdings. Mr Wilson may have exaggerated his ability to bring off such a tacit deal, but it is a tragedy that the problem should have presented itself in these terms. For so long as they keep off economic or class matters, MPs such as Michael Foot as well as others on the literary and artistic left, speak for much of what is best in British life. They have an instinctive sympathy for those who are subject to the whim of others—the conscript soldier, the prisoner in the dock, the Latin-American peasant—and they voice a very necessary rage against those who would ban and beat what they are jealous of, or do not understand.

It is a misfortune that the Left spoils its case, not only by an unnecessary linkage with fundamentalist socialism at home, but by an old-fashioned overestimation of Britain's power in the world. This is one factor which prevented it from making common cause with those Conservative MPs (far too few in number) who had qualms about unqualified support for the Vietnam war in its fiercest phase. If the Labour Left had been a little more cynical towards some British 'peace initiatives,' such as the Harold Davies Mission of 1965, and seen them for what they were—as something in between a Walter Mitty dream and cynical diversions to keep back-benchers happy—there might have been some opening for a link with those Conservative and other non-socialist doubters who would have been happier to see Britain not taking sides at all. But the Prime Minister had only to ask whether he was wrong to take the initiative to have the desired lusty partisan cheering from the benches behind him.

Indeed the worst possible environment for criticism of official attitudes is when a nominally left-wing government is in power pursuing ultra-conventional foreign and economic policies, as the Labour Government was in its first three years of office.

Dissent by critics within the Labour Party is then categorised as the outpourings of far-out 'Clause 4' types. On the other hand non-Socialist critics have an almost impossible task urging policies which seem to go further than even a Labour Government is prepared to move. The left–right mythology prevents Conservatives from recognising that there may be points of substance in what the Labour Parliamentary rebels are saying, because according to this absurd scale they are to the 'left' of Mr Wilson and therefore even further beyond the pale. A less doctrinaire examination would suggest that sometimes the Left were talking sense—as over unemployment and Vietnam in 1966–7; but at other times—such as when they opposed the policies required for making devaluation work in 1968–9—they deserved most of what was said against them.

The fear of extremes also works the other way. In 1964–7 there was a great deal of common ground between the complaints of the Labour rebels and some of the things Enoch Powell was saying or hinting on East of Suez, the pound, Vietnam, and Incomes Policy. Yet neither side would have dreamt of making common cause with the other. So long as dissent is fragmented in this way, no effective challenge can be presented, and all who disagree with official priorities can be written off by political pundits as extremists removed from 'the centre.'

Some friendly critics who saw the above passage in draft maintain that even where the Labour Left (or Tory Right) has come to sensible conclusions it has been for the wrong reasons. This is not, to my mind, a convincing argument for ostracising it. Many Gaitskellites, moderate Tories, or Liberals have come to sensible conclusions for the wrong reasons. If co-operation were confined to those who agreed in their reasoning as well as in their conclusions it would not be possible to run a political system at all.

The question has also been raised whether the fragmentation of opposition to official policy among dissidents in the two parties, who would not be seen dead in each other's company, does any great harm. Cannot as much influence be exerted by separate and unrelated campaigns within the two parties? This can be answered by observing the successes achieved on those issues where for one reason or another the left–right mythology did not operate. The EEC is perhaps the leading example where the willingness of prominent members of both parties to work together in a common campaign helped to secure support for British application for membership. On the other side of the fence, the fact that the Conservative Common Market doubters were not afraid to associate themselves with Mr Gaitskell's reservations had a large, and perhaps fatal, effect on the whole tempo of the Government's approach in 1961–3. On a very different issue, pressure from a group of Conservative MPs combined with the hostility of the Labour Opposition, forced Henry Brooke to amend the 1957 Rent Act. The fact that Labour's campaign on rents came from the whole of the party, and could not be written off as left-wing or extreme, made the Conservative rebels less worried about working in the same direction.

These are the exceptions. In most cases the myth of the left–right spectrum fragments the dissenters' forces and thereby renders them less effective. An example was provided not long ago by Dr Richard Pryke, who resigned from the Cabinet Office in 1966 and subsequently wrote a book entitled *Though Cowards Flinch*.[4] Its central theme was an attack on the overriding priority for so long given in Downing Street to preserving a supposed special relationship with the USA, to the defence of the then exchange rate, and maintaining a world role. Now there are a few Conservatives (and many more intelligent non-Socialists in the country at large) who would also have objected to some or all of these priorities. But the language in which the book was written, as well as the inclusion of extraneous material of a more traditionally Socialist kind, seemed deliberately designed to limit support to self-consciously left-wing Socialists. Similarly, those on the right who were challenging official priorities on these subjects were conducting a private argument with their colleagues, and the last people they were trying to woo were the Labour dissidents. Despite the disunity among the dissenters official policy can and does change, as it already has on some of the subjects mentioned. But the country suffers because the changes are too late, and come in response to events instead of anticipating them. It also suffers from an emotional shock when dogmas implanted by years of cross-bench indoctrination are suddenly shattered by events.

This revulsion from the extremes also does harm within Conservative ranks—mostly among the more liberal section of the Party. As good a political writer as Professor Richard Rose can list support of private bus services, to compete with public transport, as a right-wing 'reactionary variant of party policy.'[5] Yet as we have seen, free-enterprise economic ideas hardly correlate at all with the left–right spectrum in the Tory Party, either historically or at present. Nevertheless, writers in the grip of the spectrum theory tend naturally to assume that the further a policy is from socialism the more right-wing it is. Conservatives who dislike their party's right wing may be influenced against an innovation that would improve public services and give a much-needed jolt to monopoly arrogance because they dread being given the label 'right wing.' One must not exaggerate. The Conservatives are a different sort of party, and take both labels and issues with less intensity than Labour. Those with a passionate interest in transport proposals would not be deterred. But there must be many non-specialist Conservatives and non-socialist members of the public who feel that they cannot support anything that smacks of denationalisation, that they must support an incomes policy and must have some belief in indicative planning if they are not to be dubbed right-wing Conservatives, a company with which they would understandably detest being associated.

For many years almost all political writers picked on opposition to the Welfare State and to trade-unionism as the hallmark of the right-wing Tory die-hard. (This follows from the *simpliste* belief that the extreme right-winger wants to put the clock back, while the moderate Conservative reluctantly accepts change which others have initiated.) No one knows the extent to which these

stereotypes were responsible for Conservative appeasement of the
unions in the decade 1951–61, and for their failure to tackle trade
union law and re-examine the foundations of the social services
during the whole of their thirteen years in office.

Left and right are far too deeply embedded in modern political
history to be abandoned lightly. The best course would be to use
them much more selectively as terms of art, on occasions when their
rich historical associations would be appropriate. The Greek
regime set up in 1967—dedicated, no doubt sincerely, to 'purity,
religion and traditional agricultural virtues,' and suppressing the
plays of Euripides in their name—has all the traditional trap-
pings of right-wing dictatorship. The Christian Society advocated
by T. S. Eliot,[6] though far from a dictatorship, was self-consciously right-wing in the sense that it was consciously and out-
spokenly opposed to liberal values. Neither kind of society was in
the least marked by any bias in favour of private enterprise or
against government intervention. Eliot's Christian Society would
'face' such problems as the 'exploitation' of labour, 'the advantages unfairly accruing to the trader,' the 'iniquity of usury'
and other capitalist sins against medieval scholasticism.

Castro's Cuba is recognisably in the tradition of left-wing
dictatorship. If the monarchy ever tried to interfere in British
politics, there would be a new left–right division in the country;
and one hopes that at least some Conservatives—if they are sincere in their present professed beliefs—would then be on the left.
The historical associations of the term would then make clear
the apparent paradox. The very richness of half-conscious associations with distant times and places, which could make left and
right such telling descriptions used with discretion on carefully
selected occasions, makes them unsuitable as an all-purpose
political measuring rod.

5 / ALTERNATIVE CLASSIFICATIONS

Nobody ever did anything very foolish except from some strong principle.

MELBOURNE

The people who are most bigoted are those who have no convictions at all.

CHESTERTON

IT IS EASIER TO SHOW THE WEAKNESSES of the accepted left–right spectrum than to suggest alternatives. One possibility, of course, would be to give up the attempt to classify either people or their attitudes. This would involve treating every issue on its own; and any description of a politician's position would consist of an unrelated set of views without any general adjectives. Such an approach would, indeed, be preferable to the present ubiquitous employment of the left–right scale. If one cannot think of a good way of classifying people it might be better to avoid it wherever possible, and to substitute individual descriptions for category labels.

Yet although this would be an improvement on the present situation, it would be a very unsatisfactory solution. The opinions of people involved in public affairs are not random assortments of coloured balls. Some people feel more closely drawn to some of their fellows than to others on whole ranges of issues. These affinities are extremely complex to describe. They may cut across parties and overlap in an intricate way; affinities with regard to the way in which problems are analysed may cut across affinities in conclusions reached; political affinities cannot always be easily separated from common class, educational, racial or religious backgrounds, or even personal friendships. Yet they can never be completely identified with such shared experiences.

Nor are these affinities merely psychological. Certain belief-systems—about personal freedom, for example—create presumptions in favour of a whole range of permissive attitudes, from legalising homosexuality to hostility towards statutory travel allowances. Such principles or attitudes are never individually sufficient for policy recommendations, both because they may clash with other principles, and because their application to particular situations may be disputable. (In the case of the Abortion Bill, certain undoubtedly libertarian MPs, such as Leo Abse, maintained that the foetus was already a human being, the destruction of which was a form of murder.) Nevertheless among those who are sufficiently sophisticated politically to have belief-systems, correlations in specific opinions—and even more in ways of approaching problems—are to be expected. The fact that politicians are often said to be inconsistent itself implies the existence of general attitudes against which the consistency of specific actions can be assessed.

Some people accept ideological groupings as facts, but deplore their existence and do everything possible to dissolve them. Their slogan is 'Treat each issue on its merits.' They believe that general principles are either useless or positively harmful. Specific judgments are not, however, made in a vacuum, but inevitably involve both broad empirical judgments on how society works and general value-judgments about the relative merits of different types of situations. The judgments of those who believe in treating each issue on its merits are likely in practice to reflect the fashion of the moment or a point of balance between conflicting belief-systems. Paradoxically, it is just because the principles of evaluation of the political 'empiricist' are likely to be vague, muddled and inconsistent that his decisions are most unlikely to be related in any predictable way to any particular set of facts. On the contrary, the conclusions drawn from the facts will vary according to the contemporary ideological climate.

The danger of putting too great a weight upon general belief-systems is that follies may be committed out of slavish adherence to doctrines which on subsequent reflection turn out to be mistaken, oversimplified or wrongly interpreted. (Vietnam and the 'containment of Communism' doctrine may be an example.) But the danger of the cool empirical style is that it leaves the discussion of principles to antediluvian extremists such as Tory officials in South-Coast constituencies or Clause 4 socialists, and that the more contemporary type of politician may simply react to events, or attempt to fight off the fuddy-duddies, without attempting a creative role of his own.

The use of the word 'pragmatism' to describe an attempt to

'judge each issue on its merits' is, incidentally, a misnomer. Pragmatism involves judging measures by how well they will serve to achieve given aims. It has nothing to do with uncertain, non-existent, or shifting aims. The word, of course, came into vogue during Mr Wilson's premiership. It is difficult to find the correct name for the quality it is meant to describe. Neither 'empiricist' nor 'opportunist' will quite do. It was a mixture of compromise and opportunism, combined during its most successful phase with a flair for minor initiatives within the broad framework of accepted official policy.

If despite, or because of, the experiences of the Wilson era we accept the inevitability of some system of political classification, the first illusion to avoid is that there is any single satisfactory measuring-rod. There is no one alternative set of polarities to replace the left–right spectrum. Even the most oversimplified way of describing a political position must be in terms of more than one dimension if it is not to be a complete distortion.

A convenient convention is to indicate the relationship between different sets of attitudes by the angle between them. If say, there is a strong connection between the degree of belligerency

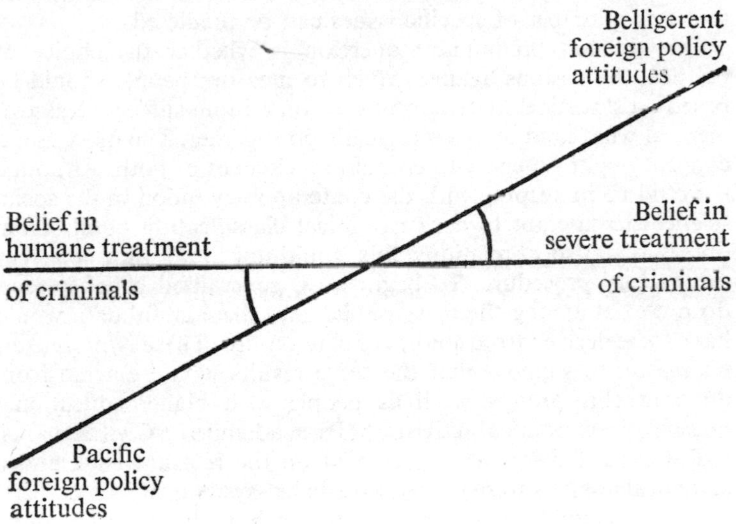

Belligerent
foreign policy
attitudes

Belief in
humane treatment

Belief in
severe treatment

of criminals

of criminals

Pacific
foreign policy
attitudes

CHART I: THE ANGLE CONVENTION

shown in foreign policy and the harshness or otherwise of views on the treatment of criminals, then attitudes on both these issues will be shown by two lines separated by a small angle. (The illustration is purely hypothetical.) Where attitudes to different subjects are regarded as unrelated, so that two entirely different dimensions are being measured, the lines are put at right-angles as in Chart 2 showing egalitarianism and liberalism. This, of course, is the usual position. Although only two dimensions can be shown conveniently on a plane diagram, there is no limit to the number of dimensions which can be envisaged if appropriate.

It would be a mistake, in my view, to take the angle convention over-literally. If two different scales are shown at right angles, this does not mean that there is believed to be absolutely no relationship between the two attitudes shown, but simply that they can be regarded as separate for the purpose of charting political attitudes. There is no intrinsic objection to using measuring-rods which are too closely related to be represented by scales at right-angles. But if we are looking for a fairly simple labelling system to replace left and right, a large number of overlapping classifications will not be helpful. For this purpose we need a very few dimensions that are relatively independent of each other, from which attitudes to a large number of specific issues can be predicted.

One difficult preliminary question is whether the choice of political dimensions against which to measure people should be based on statistical investigations, or on a more subjective assessment of what kind of views logically go together. The most useful concept ought probably to contain an element of both. Although it would be in keeping with the contemporary mood in the social sciences to attempt to derive political classification purely from observed statistical relations, this would not in my view be a very satisfactory procedure. To begin with, generalised belief-systems do not exist among the mass public, and meaningful data would have to be derived from studies of elite groups. There is, moreover, no reason to suppose that the same results would emerge from different elite groups, such as people with higher educational qualifications, political activists, M Ps, academics or Civil Servants.

But even if there were agreement on the relevant elite, and a statistical analysis were made of the belief-systems of its members, there would still be no compulsion to accept without argument the classification that emerged. If it so happened, for instance, that anti-egalitarians tended to be authoritarian because they were brought up in old-fashioned public schools, a high positive correlation between the two attitudes might be obtained. But this does not show that the two attitudes are intrinsically related, and there is no reason why a liberal should not be an anti-egalitarian.

The opposite approach would be for the political analyst to start out with the dimensions which he personally thinks important, but separate, and rank people's views along them. The difficulty here is that there is no limit to the number of rival systems of political classification that writers can invent and even find support for in the historical record. As Philip Converse has hinted, a vast number of different permutations of beliefs on different subjects have at one time or another been grouped together by different political movements. Among some ascetic religious sects plain living has been linked, with apparent logic, to an abhorrence of technological progress. Among others such progress has been highly prized, for apparently equally cogent reasons.[1]

There would seem to be two ways out of this *impasse*. One would be to make a subjective choice in the light of the main currents of Western political thinking that seem most relevant, but to make sure that the dimensions so selected pass certain empirical tests. The main necessary condition for any usable classification, as has already been suggested in Chapter 3, is its ability to predict how a person, or group, will react to new issues, or fresh twists to old issues. The second approach would be to start at the other end with a statistical investigation but also satisfy oneself that the postulated links between views on different subjects are not simply due to archaic survivals or to mistaken thinking, but have some more defensible connection.

It may help to explain what I have in mind if I indicate at this point (and justify later) the very tentative classification I am suggesting in place of left and right. This uses three different axes along which people or groups are to be classified. They are:

(a) Egalitarianism versus elitism
(b) Radicalism versus orthodoxy
(c) Liberalism versus authoritarianism.

The first dimension most nearly corresponds to the residue of meaning in left and right. In Charts 2, 3 and 4 I have 'placed' a few illustrative names and groups, but purely as a *jeu d'esprit*

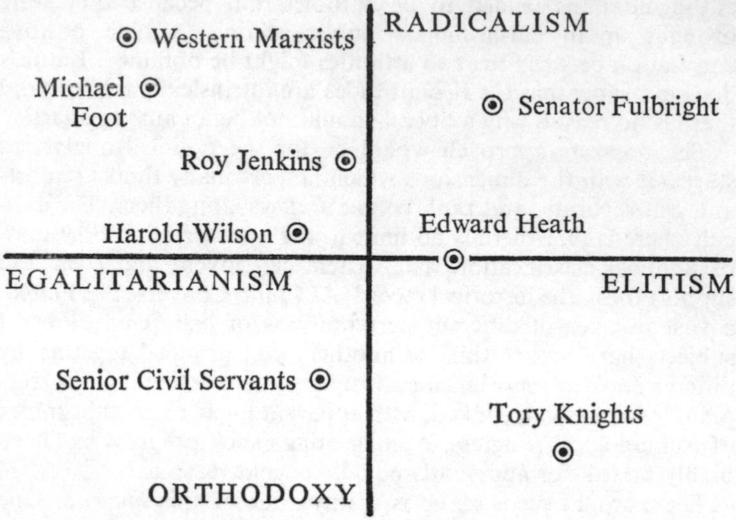

⊙ Western Marxists | RADICALISM

Michael ⊙
Foot

⊙ Senator Fulbright

Roy Jenkins ⊙

Harold Wilson ⊙   Edward Heath
                            ⊙
EGALITARIANISM _____ ELITISM

Senior Civil Servants ⊙

Tory Knights
⊙

ORTHODOXY

CHART 2: EGALITARIANISM AND RADICALISM

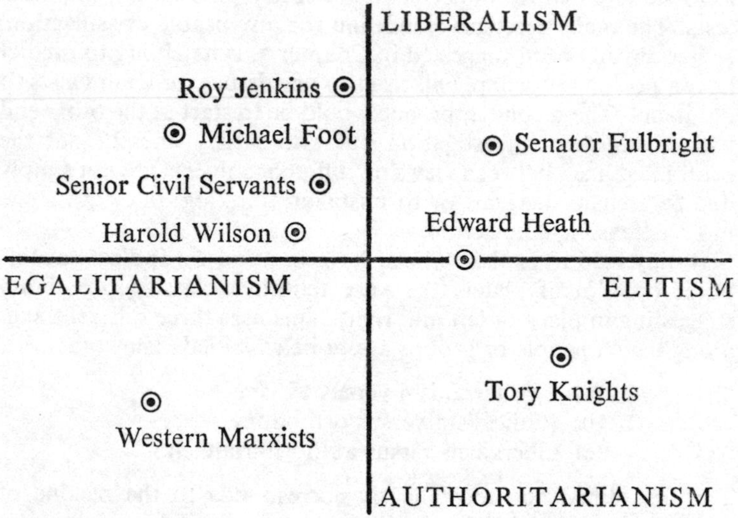

LIBERALISM

Roy Jenkins ⊙
⊙ Michael Foot   ⊙ Senator Fulbright
Senior Civil Servants ⊙
Harold Wilson ⊙   Edward Heath
                            ⊙
EGALITARIANISM _____ ELITISM

⊙
Tory Knights

⊙
Western Marxists

AUTHORITARIANISM

CHART 3: EGALITARIANISM AND LIBERALISM

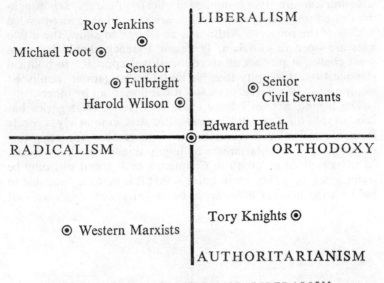

CHART 4: RADICALISM AND LIBERALISM

The last thing I want to suggest is that people can be adequately classified by means of these stock labels. My point simply is that where an all-purpose description is unavoidable, the three suggested axes would be an improvement on left and right alone. There are of course many situations which they would not cover; and later in the chapter I suggest other polarities for use on particular occasions.

Many readers will notice that my suggested descriptive system is an elaboration and modification of one put forward by Professor H. J. Eysenck, which is by far the best-known alternative classification to left and right in this country.[3] This was derived from statistical investigations originally among W E A classes, but later extended to other groups and other countries. Eysenck classifies people along two axes at right-angles to each other (illustrated in Chart 5). One axis goes from radicalism on the left to conservatism on the right; and the other from tender-mindedness at the bottom to tough-mindedness at the top. (To give the flavour of this classification to those who have not come across it:

Communists are tough-minded radicals, Fascists are tough-minded conservatives, and Liberals are somewhat tender-minded middle-of-the-roaders.) Although, as I hope to show, these two axes are open to criticism, Professor Eysenck should be given great credit for pioneering the dimensional approach to political classification. It is a pity that his initial investigations, published as long ago as 1954, has been so little followed up by others.

The biggest change I have made in Eysenck's categories has been to split off a new egalitarian–elitist axis, completely separate from his radical–conservative one. The reasons for regarding radicalism and egalitarianism as highly distinct qualities today, have been given at length in Chapters 2 and 3, and will only be summarised here. The main point is that it is perfectly possible to hold a large number of iconoclastic or 'advanced' views without

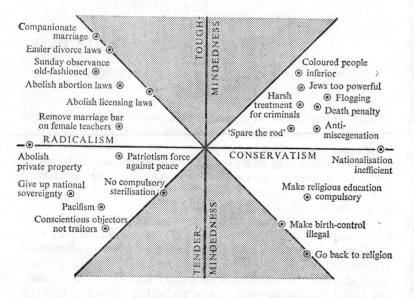

CHART 5: THE EYSENCK CLASSIFICATION: DISTRIBU-
TION OF ATTITUDES WITH RESPECT TO TOUGH-
MINDEDNESS AND RADICALISM
(*Reproduced by permission of Routledge and Kegan Paul and Professor Eysenck*)

being an egalitarian (still less a socialist). People of this kind will not be entirely welcome in either party. In the Labour Party they are forced to be hypocrites; in the Conservative Party the path of the non-conformist is a thorny one. Yet there are many non-egalitarians who take a delight in challenging cherished beliefs and conventional assumptions. The fact that these attitudes may some-times be cocktail-party affectations, or attempts to be 'amusing,' does not invalidate the distinction. Radical attitudes *can* be sincerely held by non-egalitarians, and quite often are. Conversely many egalitarians are profoundly unradical—the trade union movement provides a wealth of examples.

The questionnaire Eysenck publishes for assessing radicalism versus conservatism has sixteen relevant items. Of these, some eight deal with punishment and social permissiveness, four with internationalism versus aggressive patriotism, and four with public versus private ownership and control. Not a single question bears directly on the egalitarian issue, and only one of the questions on public versus private enterprise issues touches marginally on it.[3] Thus one cannot say that th egalitarian issue is already comprehended in the radical axis.

Indirect support for the distinction between egalitarianism and radicalism is provided by Eysenck's own observation that working-class supporters of a given political party tend to be less radical than middle-class supporters.[4] Eysenck mentions a hypothesis that there are two kinds of conservatism, one concerning economic matters and the other 'ideational' subjects, and that middle-class people are economically conservative, while working-class people are 'ideationally' conservative. He attempts to refute this hypo-thesis by pointing out that middle-class respondents more frequently call for the abolition of private property than working-class ones! This is not so surprising. The abolition of private property is a highly abstract slogan which made little appeal to workers in the late 1940s and early 1950s. The workers' lack of interest in the more extreme socialist ideology of the period does not invalidate the hypothesis that there is a class-related cluster of vaguely egalitarian attitudes which might have made consider-able appeal to them if couched in simple everyday terms.

A more potent criticism of my suggested egalitarian–elitist axis would be that it is a mixture of two different concepts—economic equality, and attitudes to 'class' in the English sense of status-groups with a strong hereditary and educational element. One could imagine societies—say nineteenth-century America— where attitudes to economic equality and to social class would have no relation and could be regarded as separate dimensions. There are many Americans who even today would be bitterly opposed to the British class system, but would also consider that rich capitalists are scandalously badly treated by the British fiscal system. (This is related to the distinction between equality of opportunity and equality of income.) But—partly as a result of the crumbling in the last decade of the old type of status barriers based on family, school or accent—attitudes towards economic and social equality are probably more closely interrelated than ever before in contemporary England. Given the degree of over-simplification necessary for any system of classification, egalitarianism versus elitism can be represented along one dimension.

A much more difficult problem is the interpretation of the radicalism axis even after it has been divested of egalitarian associations. As radicalism challenges traditional attitudes, the content of radical policies must change over the years. Yet radicalism is itself a tradition; and the tendency to adopt the latest and most superficial fad is surely not the one we are trying to locate. 'Radicalism' has become such a hold-all catch-phrase that it would, indeed be tempting to jettison it altogether. Unfortunately, there is no other word which will quite take its place. Within a Cabinet of either party a man who tends to reject the advice of his officials for properly thought-out reasons, who disbelieves in traditional religion and morality, who successfully reforms his own department and its policies, and who is sceptical of the accepted Western version of the East-West conflict, differs from his more conventional colleagues; there is no better word than radicalism to describe his whole collection of attitudes.

But such clear-cut cases as the one invented in the previous paragraph are infrequent, to say the least. What is normally labelled radicalism may comprise one or more of a number of different attitudes. It may comprise an optimistic belief in the possibility of human improvement and a consequent zeal for reform. This variant of radicalism is very far from being a platitudinously correct position for any intelligent person of goodwill. It is very different from the approach of most theologians, historians or of many great writers. For it leaves out original sin, or, in another terminology, takes an optimistic view of people's ability to overcome the historical and unconscious forces impeding the rational approach.

A more borderline type of attitude would be political activism, not necessarily connected with any very great optimism about human improvement, but undertaken out of restlessness, ambition, or a belief that action is required to prevent deterioration. But provided the actions taken are genuinely far-reaching and not just publicity devices, they have a claim to be regarded as radical in this sense. Two leading examples would be the rapid liquidation of empire carried out by both Harold Macmillan and General de Gaulle—probably more rapid than Socialist leaders would have carried out in their place.

In another of its nuances radicalism involves a highly rational attitude to hallowed and traditional beliefs—in contemporary jargon a rejection of 'sacred cows.' The problem here is how to class someone whose scepticism towards traditional beliefs is not accompanied by any zeal to change the world and who may be equally sceptical towards the ideals of the reformers. The Scottish philosopher David Hume was a good example of this combination. So too was Lord Salisbury, who led the Conservatives at the end of the nineteenth century. Lord Salisbury was among the most *immobiliste* of British Prime Ministers and, unlike his predecessor Disraeli, abominated all the contemporary reform movements. Yet in many ways his cast of mind was much nearer that of the radicals than it was to the conventional Tories of his time, with whom he felt ill at ease. He had no veneration for hallowed institutions. His standards of judgment were entirely utilitarian and he actually used the Benthamite phraseology of the greatest happiness. His early comments on colonisation were scathing (e.g. 'seizing a coloured man's land and giving it to a white man'). He believed war to be the ultimate evil and the avoidance of it the main aim of foreign policy. He criticised the law courts for their lack of support for freedom of the press. He debunked ceremonies such as the Opening of Parliament; he attacked both the classical curriculum and corporal punishment at public schools. He differed from the radicals in believing that political 'reform' was usually a change for the worse; the fault he condemned above all others was optimism and he praised Palmerston's Ministry for doing 'that which it is most difficult and salutary for a Parliament to do—

nothing.'[5] Perhaps the contemporary politician who has (lately at least) moved nearest this intellectual combination is Reginald Maudling.

There is yet another form of radicalism more closely connected with the etymological derivation of the word, i.e. an insistence on getting to the root of the matter. This is usually taken to involve a great stress on logical analysis in both diagnosis and treatment, and frequently leads to intellectual extremism. Perhaps the leading contemporary example would be one kind of academic economist. Instead of supporting such worthy causes as the Export Drive or the Back Britain campaign, he might ask why market forces have not automatically made it profitable to export as much as we need to keep our overseas account in balance; this may lead to shocking heresies, such as the view that all these worthy activities are really pernicious and would be quite unnecessary with a free exchange rate and proper control of home demand.

So far the emphasis has been on radicalism as an approach, rather than as a fixed body of beliefs. This is broadly correct, but there is some stratum of content as well. Most varieties of radicalism usually involve some commitment to hedonism; for reason does not set its own ends, and it is characteristic of the radical to be unconvinced by arguments for either higher or lower ends than the pursuit of one's own or other people's happiness. It is often said that the heresies of one generation become the orthodoxies of the next. This aphorism is only three-quarters true. There are some originally heretical doctrines which never quite settle down in their subsequent orthodox role. However much they appear to be accepted there often has to be a shadow repeat of old engagements before they are actually followed in real situations; and victory is not always assured. Keynesian economics, 'progressive' educational ideas, sexual permissiveness and religious disbelief, to take four examples from different spheres, still retain a trace of their radical origin. Respectable opinion is still not at ease with the 'new orthodoxies,' however much it labels them as such.

It would nevertheless be wrong to search for a single feature common to all the different varieties of radicalism. For what they have in common is what Wittgenstein aptly called 'family resemblances.' Each member of a family will have resemblances in one or other respect to some of the other members, although it will always be possible to find members between whom there is no resemblance whatever. Or as Wittgenstein put it in another metaphor, 'the strength of the thread does not reside in the fact that some one fibre runs through its whole length, but in the overlapping of many fibres.'[6]

The great variety of specific policy views that can accompany a radical approach is brought out in Charts 2 and 4, where Senator Fulbright, Roy Jenkins and Michael Foot are all shown towards the radical end. (The opposite end of the axis has been rechristened as orthodoxy, which is a more apt name than Eysenck's 'conservatism.') This grouping of different political positions does not destroy the validity of the axis. The distinction between Foot, Jenkins and Fulbright emerges strongly enough on the egalitarian dimension in Charts 2 and 3. The point of the common classification can be seen by comparing them with Mr Wilson and Mr Heath, who are both near the centre. (Mr Macmillan was more radical than either present-day party leader, but still within sight of the centre.) Senior Civil Servants are often found fairly far over on the orthodox side. On the whole front-benchers are less radical than their own Young Turks, but much more radical than dedicated party supporters, who do not possess the knowledge of the reforms that are really required, but have a strong emotional investment in generalised party slogans.

With any classification, there are some people who cannot be satisfactorily placed on it at all. This applies here to the 'radical-reactionaries,' such as Goldwater in 1964 or Cobbett in the early nineteenth century. There are undoubtedly some features common to the radical-reactionaries and some members of the radical family—above all the wish to change a great deal. But the degree of kinship is so remote that they must in my view be placed outside the boundaries of the radical family. (A detailed analysis of the views of Enoch Powell would show how difficult it can sometimes be to know where to draw the boundary line.)

So much for radical versus orthodox. The other main change I have made in Eysenck's classification has been the replacement of his tough–tender-minded axis by a liberal versus authoritarian one, as the reader will appreciate if he compares Chart 5 with Charts 2, 3, and 4. The underlying idea behind Professor Eysenck's tough-minded–tender-minded axis has, of course, a great deal to be said for it. It does mark out common characteristics shared by the hanger and flogger, and the revolutionary who would walk through rivers of blood. At the other end of the scale it brings together the type of Conservative whose views are governed by a horror of war or revolution and the humane reformer. It is interesting that some of the pre-war Conservative appeasers were both, including R. A. Butler and Sir Samuel Hoare of the Hoare–Laval Pact, who as Lord Templewood later established a reputation for himself as a reforming Home Secretary.

Nevertheless there are severe objections to the particular axis suggested by Eysenck. To begin with, the nomenclature is unfortunate. 'Tough-mindedness' in one of its most frequent meanings is an intellectual virtue, and one which any intelligent reformer, however humane, would aspire to possess. Muddled wishful thinking is as self-defeating as hard-boiled cynicism for anyone who wants to make human life more pleasant. The danger of the label is that stress on intellectual rigour, and a harsh, punitive attitude towards other human beings, will seem to share a common label.

The word 'tough' itself has become much overworked and is well due for a rest. (In many ways it is even more objectionable than right and left.) In its correct use it confuses two very different qualities. Physical and mental resilience on the part of leaders are regarded as signs of toughness, as are the unpleasant measures a leader may impose on others. The ambiguity of the term allows admiration that is felt for the former qualities to be transferred to the latter. Tough policies may mean policies that take courage to introduce; they may mean painful policies; it is a masochistic myth that the two always go together. The whole concept of toughness is not merely descriptive, but embodies the equation political leadership = realism = ruthlessness, which is as untrue as it is repellent. Even used in its physical sense to describe individuals, the concept is an utterly charmless one. Has even the most 'with-it' translator of the classics dared to suggest that Greek heroes were 'tough'? Add qualities of endurance to the Appollonic attributes by all means, but dispense with that dreadful adjective, which probably owes its vogue to the ease with which it can be fitted into newspaper headlines ('Tough Policies Will Stay—P.M.').

More important than any misgivings about labels are the objections to Eysenck's criteria for placing people on this scale. Few of those who only know the names 'tough-minded' and 'tender-minded,' but have not actually filled in the relevant questionnaire, would guess that belief in easier divorce, companionate marriage, abortion reform or euthanasia count as tough-minded. So do *opposition* to compulsory Sunday observance and to the present licensing laws. All such permissive beliefs count in the same direction as a belief in corporal punishment, compulsory military training, and treating conscientious objectors as traitors. At the other end of the scale, not only do pacifism and opposition to blood sports count as tender-minded, so too do the opinions that birth control, except when recommended by a doctor, should be made illegal, and that religious education should be compulsory.

Indeed every pro-religious, pro-Church and theologically conservative view seems to count as tender-minded, irrespective of its other qualities. A tough-minded hanger and flogger is brought back towards the centre, and perhaps even to the tender-minded side, if he is also a religious man who believes in beating the devil out of offenders; and his ranking may not differ from that of a soft-hearted humanist, whose score has been reduced because of his religious disbelief. This unqualified equation of pro-religious replies with tender-mindedness seems to me highly misguided. The doctrine of original sin has often bred extremely hard and insensitive attitudes. There is the tradition of the Inquisition as well as of St Francis. Anyone who has seen the statue of St Paul, sword in hand, outside the Church of St Paulo fuori le Mura in Rome, will hesitate before automatically classifying the religious believer as tender-minded.

These objections cannot be answered by saying that the attitudes classified by Eysenck as tough-minded and tender-minded go together empirically, whether we like it or not. On the contrary Eysenck's own data suggest that his tough-minded category brings together two entirely different kinds of attitudes, as does his tender-minded category. This can be demonstrated by means of his own basic diagram shown in Chart 5.* It will be seen that the

* The choice of the nationalisation–private-property issue to represent radicalism versus conservatism should not disturb readers. It is probably explained by the fact that the data were largely collected in the post-1945 period. In addition Eysenck's radicalism–conservatism axis is intentionally much more closely linked to Labour–Conservative differences than my own suggested radical–orthodox classification, from which the egalitarian dimension has been removed.

permissive kind of 'tough-mindedness,' involving easier abortion and the reform of the licensing laws, is shown at right-angles to the hanging and flogging sort of tough-mindedness. This indicates that no connection between them was shown in Eysenck's statistical studies. Indeed the angle between them is actually rather more than 90°, which suggests that social permissiveness is, if anything, more likely to be associated with opposition to harsh or punitive attitudes. Similarly there is a 90° angle or more between the pacifist, dove-like kind of tender-mindedness and the religious-authoritarian variety.

Even more remarkable, not a single attitude shown on the diagram lies anywhere near (in fact anywhere less than 45° from) the tough–tender axis. This is a point of which Eysenck himself is very well aware, and he goes out of his way to stress it.[7] Direct inspection of the diagram suggests that the social attitudes in question can be much more convincingly mapped if the tough–tender axis is replaced by the two dotted lines shown in the diagram (placed there by Eysenck himself), running from north-east to south-west and from north-west to south-east. Rotated in this way the two axes are at once recognisable. South-west to north-east is a hawk-dove axis running from pacifism at one end to harsh treatment of criminals and alien peoples at the other. The north-west to south-east axis represents a scale of social permissiveness, with easier divorce and abortion at one end and compulsory religious education at the other.

Eysenck discusses the arguments for and against these alternative axes at some length. The basic reason why he prefers the hypothetical construct of tough- versus tender-minded is that he believes that such a classification is directly related to more basic personality traits such as extraversion and introversion, and perhaps even to neural phenomena.[8] These are essentially psychological rather than political questions on which I would not venture to express an opinion. For the purpose of political description with which this chapter is concerned the hawk–dove and permissiveness axes seem more relevant.

My own liberal–authoritarian dimension has its origin in the permissiveness dimension as it emerges from the Eysenck diagram; but it is extended to cover a much wider range of issues between liberty and authority. It includes not merely traditional questions about the limits of political freedom, but also economic ones, such as freedom to try out a new business venture and freedom of consumer choice.*

One reason why I have used only the liberal–authoritarian axis on Chart 2 and jettisoned the dove–hawk contrast is simply a desire to avoid a fourth dimension. But there are some positive reasons for my choice. The conflict between liberty and authority is, as Mill pointed out, one of the most durable of political issues, extending from the earliest records of Greece and Rome to the present age. In addition it would almost certainly cut across, practically at right-angles, the egalitarian dimension; and, extended in the way suggested, would probably be reasonably independent in contemporary conditions of attitudes to radicalism. Moreover, a sufficiently liberal position on this axis is also—because of its non-interventionist implications—some safeguard against oppressive authority. But only some; one should not forget the hawk-like liberal who would inflict the most draconian punishments for the slightest interference with private property. The dove–hawk contrast must be kept in reserve.

Liberalism is itself a term that has been enormously stretched to cover a great many attitudes widely separated from the belief in personal freedom it was originally intended to convey. An American liberal, in particular, often has a bias towards state authority in domestic issues; while in Britain the word is often used as a vague term of commendation. One is tempted to substitute the word 'individualism.' But it is better not to do so, because the term often carries with it an additional suggestion of strong conservatism, and also because it more often implies a belief in the unrestrained use of the force of one's own personality than a respect for the freedom of others.

Any attempt to reduce individual views and issues to three dimensions as in Charts 2–4 must inevitably be very rough and ready. There will always be room for argument about both the interpretation of the scales and the exact position of people on them. (One could argue indefinitely about whether Mr Heath was slightly more or slightly less radical than Mr Wilson.) While

---

* Roy Jenkins retains his position near the liberal end of this axis despite the Government's prices and incomes policy because his *intention* in this sphere is not anti-libertarian and the long-term *effects* of any kind are likely to be minor. To justify these assertions adequately would require a long economic digression out of place in this essay.

it would be absurd to take the charts too seriously, I would claim that the ideas they embody are an improvement on left and right alone; and they are put forward, very tentatively with that intent. It should not be too difficult for political writers to use three adjectives instead of one in their standard descriptions, and I am sure that convenient monosyllables can in time be found to replace cumbersome words such as egalitarian or authoritarian.

Even on an oversimplified basis, there will always be some political personalities who cannot be placed, on either one or all of the axes. This will apply not only to people of subtle or original views, but also to those who are liable to jump in any direction on any issue, and whose approach to specific questions cannot be predicted from underlying dispositions because they hardly have any. To say that a politician cannot be classified is not, therefore, invariably a compliment. To play fair with the reader I ought to mention at this point that I regard myself as moderately, but only moderately, on the radical side of the radical–conservative axis, well on the liberal side of the liberal–authoritarian one and absolutely dead centre on the egalitarian scale. (The latter statement is a way of expressing my extreme disagreement with both the ideal of equality and the rival ideal of inequality.)

It is most desirable that the usefulness of these three axes should be tested empirically. Such empirical investigations will never themselves supply a ready answer on a plate. The picture they are most likely to show is Terence's 'Quot homines tot sententiae'— as many opinions as men—with very little obvious pattern. Even statistical analysis of relationships will, judging by precedent, most likely reveal a large number of fairly modest correlations between attitudes on different subjects, leaving the investigator to impose some order. The main help that such research could give would be to place a constraint on imaginative constructions of the kind I have attempted. If it were found, for example, that there was an inverse relation between different attitudes on the liberalism scale, so that people who were against the Travel Allowance or state control of wages and prices nearly always favoured anti-homo-sexuality laws and theatre censorship, we might have to conclude regretfully that the liberalism scale was untenable. But before accepting any such conclusion it would be desirable to see if these negative conclusions prevailed among people with *roughly the same ratings on the other axes*, above all the egalitarian one.

Statistical testing could also ascertain if there were ways of measuring egalitarianism, radicalism and liberalism, which would make them relatively independent of each other. These scales, it must be emphasised, could not be meaningfully used on the mass public and are relevant only to the politically informed elite.*

Three scales have been suggested for the purpose of a standard classification. But there are many other useful polarities which will on particular occasions be relevant. The dove–hawk classification has already been discussed. The description of 'reactionary' ought to be mentioned here. The normal definition, in terms of a desire to go back to some past order, does not convey its whole flavour: a strong mixture of repressive harshness is usually involved as well. Reaction in common usage is a compound of hawkishness and authoritarianism, plus a desire to put the clock back. As such it is a good hate word which could often be substituted for the pejorative sense of 'right-wing.' The opposite of reactionary is, I suppose 'progressive,' a term so abused that it is most often used ironically in quotation marks.

Another very important polarity is asceticism (or puritanism) versus hedonism. This distinction has occurred in different forms on many different occasions, such as the Roundheads versus Cavaliers, or the distinction once made between the aldermanic and the buccaneering type of Tory (the latter type being much out of favour in the present-day Conservative Party). A further interesting dimension relates to how seriously the whole world of public affairs is taken. At one end we find Leo Tolstoy, and in our own day Malcolm Muggeridge or A. J. P. Taylor, who enjoy exposing the vanity of people's pretensions—for example how little it matters if X or Y is appointed Minister or General, or what he decides. Events are decided by impersonal forces, chance or original sin. At the other extreme are those who attach enormous importance to the form and content of every Whitehall or party committee, and have no eye for the absurdity of most of the ritual of party politics.

* After all the testing the classification would still remain an imaginative construction, subject to empirical constraints. The discussion of the possibility of rotating the axes in Eysenck's diagram shows that even a highly complex technique such as factor analysis leaves a large degree of freedom to choose the dimensions which are thought to be politically interesting. Facts cannot speak for themselves; they have to be made to speak, although there is a limit on what they can be made to say.

Here again one can be misled by appearances. The jovial figure, who is careful never to look too intense, may be very credulous about the importance of political trivia, while the earnest-looking bespectacled type may be very conscious of how little it all matters. In this context taking political activities seriously is a first cousin of taking oneself seriously; and those who are incapable of taking a detached attitude towards their own careers and ambitions are likely to find themselves on the serious side of the spectrum. The interesting feature of this classification is that, in private conversation at least, the competition would be for the less serious side, with most people trying to pretend to be less involved than they really are.

A straight-line ranking would hide some of the more interesting nuances of this distinction. It is not merely that some people take political processes (or themselves) more seriously than others. Most people have their individual obsessions. With some it is the details of procedures or wording of statements; with some it is the immediate task they happen to be on; with others it is the political speech. There are those who overestimate the minutiae of policy and those who overstress the importance of the Party Leader's activities. (The Prime Minister may have gone to India or to Newcastle to 'see things for himself,' an activity which may be very illuminating for the man concerned but of doubtful relevance to the nation's affairs.)

Another measuring rod worth investigating is humanism. The opposition here is between the Greek exaltation of man as the measure of all things, and the type of medieval Christianity which regarded human life as of no account except as a preparation for the world to come. It would be interesting to rank modern politicians, movements and regimes according to the degree to which they share the Greek and Renaissance concern for the glory of the individual human being, the body as well as the spirit. It would also be worth investigating whether the classical-romantic dichotomy can be applied to the wider world of political action.

One can go on adding indefinitely to the polarities. For example there is a rebelliousness–conformity axis, which would have a positive correlation with the radicalism axis but would be far from identical with it. This is not only an amusing game, but a useful exercise in bringing out the vast range of human differences, relevant to politics, which are smothered out of existence by current clichés.

There are all the same important aspects of a person's political position which cannot be presented, even in oversimplified terms, on a straight line. The leading example is the complex of issues related to race and nation. One could define a spectrum of xenophobia, in which dislike of foreigners and racial prejudices would score highly. But most politically active people would take care to receive a low rating here. The xenophobic axis is not necessarily the same thing as belligerency in international affairs; and the latter is not the same as readiness to subordinate the individual to the state, either because of some sophistical philosophy à la Hegel or in the supposed interest of national security. The state in this context is almost a disembodied entity concerned with foreign policy as an end in itself. It is not the same as the state in the sense of general community to which some socialists want individuals to be subjected, although the two notions come together in regimes like Stalin's Russia. Internationalism versus Little Englandism is again a different concept. Internationalism is not necessarily the opposite of war; 'outward-looking' adherents not only of UNO, but more significantly of NATO, the Common Market, and even the Central Bankers, capitalise on the pacific connotations of the word internationalism to generate support for themselves.

What are we to say of the opposing school which wants to put Britain's own self-interest first? In contemporary terms this is likely to mean *less* military action, less dying for one's country, than the good Atlanticist would advocate. Yet some of the younger Conservative politicians who support such policies might use a nationalist terminology which Labour and Liberal advocates would find embarrassing. Is one to say there is a cross-bench alignment, disguised by differences in terminology? Or is the alliance an entirely ephemeral one, with utterly different motives behind the participants. It is impossible to say. The Conservatives in question like to pride themselves on their realism; and it is anyone's guess how they would react if some form of gunboat diplomacy were to become again a feasible form of nationalism.

It would be best not even to try to reduce the whole set of issues involving nationalism to dimensional form. Some hint of readiness to subordinate the individual to the nation-state can be given along the liberalism axis; an impression of how likely a person is to accept the duty to 'die for his country,' without analysing the concept, can be given along the radicalism axis. The most relevant dimension would, however, be the subsidiary one of 'hawks' versus 'doves.' But great care would have to be employed in using it. There can still be debate about how far Neville Chamberlain was a real dove, and how far he was credulous towards Hitler in a way he would never have been towards a Communist dictatorship.

Most of the classifications so far considered in this chapter, although more illuminating than left and right alone, are too general to predict where a man will stand on many of the complex policy issues on which Civil Servants and Ministers spend much of their time. There is something to be said for supplementing them by more transitory political classifications that group the key questions of the period in an illuminating way.

One leading example of what I have in mind is relevant to differences between successive Chancellors, which appear to cut across party and other distinctions. Just as in the nineteenth century every boy and girl was born 'either a little Liberal or else a little Conservative' today every economist is born a little inflationist or deflationist. Most sensible economists of either school would want to curb inflationary and deflationary excesses; and they would often agree with each other on the need for action long before the politicians or bankers see a problem. But in the large area of judgment which remains after all the arguments have been considered, one set of economists is temperamentally more worried about inflation, the other about recession and unemployment. It is easy enough to see that Thorneycroft and Selwyn Lloyd stood on one side of the fence and Butler and Maudling on the other; differences in circumstances do not wholly explain the matter away. (It is too early to classify Roy Jenkins, but I would tend to put him in the second category despite his 1968 Budget.)

The vital disagreements are not really about trade-cycle management at all. The economist with a deflationary bias believes in keeping people on their toes by maintaining some slack, so that orders are difficult to get and jobs not over-plentiful. The other school of thought puts more emphasis on an expansionary climate, with some labour shortages as an inducement to expand and innovate. These are not matters which can on present evidence be resolved by objective analysis. Moreover if it turned out that either approach, *consistently applied*, could be a success the choice between them would be a matter of taste. There is almost certainly some correlation between the inflationist-deflationist and the hedonist–ascetic scales.

There is, however, a much wider classification linking foreign and economic policy. For a number of years the most relevant underlying division among British policy makers has related to 'Atlanticism,' or in more popular terms the extent to which we should try to preserve a 'special relationship' with the USA. Until the devaluation and the associated policy reappraisal at the end of 1967, it was easy to set out a recognisable Atlanticist syndrome: public support for American policies towards the Communist world (combined sometimes with a belief that these policies can best be influenced by private remonstrance); support for the Common Market as a step towards Atlantic Union, and an interest in a North Atlantic Free Trade Area as an alternative; belief in an East-of-Suez military role for Britain; hostility towards a change in the price of gold, and determined support for both the sterling area and the sterling exchange rate.

It would be absurd to argue that anyone who was an Atlanticist on some of these issues would have been an Atlanticist on all of them. There was nevertheless a close, though imperfect, correlation of attitudes among those who took the Atlanticist line—which was also in a very meaningful sense the establishment line. Those who both wanted Britain to play a world role and to do so as America's trusted partner, desired also to supplement US efforts at containing 'Communism' in Asia. Sterling and the sterling area were supported both as a financial reflection of Britain's world role and because it was believed that any change would bring down the dollar. The Foreign Office was passionately devoted to an 'outward-looking' Europe—by which it meant a Europe which would not diverge too far from the USA; it was reluctant to reduce British overseas commitments and it was the fount-head of the concept of the 'special relationship' with America. (This showed itself in all sorts of interesting little ways. American correspondents in London were given special private briefings of their own, apart from other 'foreign' journalists.)

Again, readiness to query one of the Atlanticist postulates

often led to querying the others. Among Conservatives a leading
anti-Atlanticist was undoubtedly Enoch Powell; he was fighting
the same negative battle, at least, as those MPs defined in a
preceding chapter as the 'Labour Left.' Anti-Atlanticists of all
political persuasions agreed to a large extent in querying Britain's
East of Suez commitments, American Asian policies and the
habit of automatically endorsing them, the refusal to devalue
until there was no choice left, and the whole Walter Mitty idea
of a private line from Downing Street to the White House.

On this range of issues the two Party Leaders were in a genuine
sense in the centre. As a result of his own experiences in Brussels
Mr Heath saw and sympathised with European aspirations for
independence from the USA, and even hinted that Britain's
military ties might be switched towards Europe.⁹ On the other
hand, he was not sufficient of an iconoclast to take a wholeheartedly anti-Atlanticist position, was a passionate and unqualified supporter of the USA in Vietnam, and temperamentally
preferred treating issues separately to grouping them in a *Weltan-
schauung*. Mr Wilson began in 1964 as the most extreme of
Atlanticists; but in 1967 there were many signs of disillusion setting
in, together with the birth of a new dream that he might one day
lead a united Europe. This drift away from Atlanticism was
accelerated by the devaluation decision, and by early 1968 he was
probably less Atlanticist than Mr Heath, though liable to shift
in either direction.

Posing the problems of British overseas policy in these terms is
undoubtedly unfair to some sections of opinion. The ex-Gaitskell-
lites were extremely pro-American and would have shuddered at
being associated with any of the attitudes of General de Gaulle
or the former Bevanite group. Nevertheless they were among the
main opponents of exaggerated ideas of Britain's world role, East
of Suez expenditure, and the vain struggle to maintain the sterling
parity. The Atlanticist dimension, moreover, never provided a
single straight line along which to rank people, unless one was to
rank the anti-Atlanticists simply by the extent of their negative
attitudes. For there were not one but many opposite poles to the
Atlanticists. There were the out-and-out Europeans, the Little
Englanders, those who believed that we could still play an important *independent* role all over the world, and those who thought
that the Commonwealth could be revived.

The argument for the Atlanticist simplification was that British post-war external policy under successive Governments exhibited a striking continuity in a characteristic set of attitudes in the most diverse fields. Indeed they went back to Churchill's three interlocking circles—the USA, Europe and the Commonwealth, with the US relationship in practice the one of which most care was taken. A discussion of the Atlanticist assumptions of successive British Prime Ministers would be extremely fruitful—and in my view would shed a great deal of light on the mistakes they made. But the mind sinks at the thought of a discussion of whether their view of Britain's role was too 'left-wing' or 'right-wing.'

The real difficulty with classifications such as Atlanticism is that by the time they are recognised they may have ceased to be appropriate. There were at the time of writing signs that this was already beginning to happen with Atlanticism itself. The catalyst that brought Atlanticism into the open as an issue was undoubtedly General de Gaulle. Many non-Atlanticists were far from being Gaullists; but the activities of the General forced many politicians in all countries of Europe to think more critically about their relations with the USA. The decline in the General's credibility that began with the Quebec visit of 1967 and the growing tendency to look beyond his reign was already blurring the issue. In Britain, the most important single prop on which the Atlanticists depended—the need for American support to preserve the pound—was knocked away on 18 November 1967 when sterling was devalued. Thus both Atlanticists and anti-Atlanticists were running out of steam. Exactly how much is left of the issue, or what might replace it as a political divide among the *cognoscenti*, is extremely difficult to predict and may not be clear for some time to come.

The aim of this inevitably complicated chapter has been to discuss alternative categories to replace a simple reliance on left and right. Dimensions such as Atlanticism, or inflationary versus deflationary bias, have the advantage of close connection with the issues which actually worry Ministers and senior officials outside their speech-making hours. But they are too transitory, limited and stratospheric in their appeal to provide a basis for a general political classification. For such purposes we need attitudes of a more permanent kind which link up more directly with people's beliefs about society. This then is the justification for the main tripartite classification suggested here in terms of egalitarianism, liberalism, radicalism and their opposites. They are offered in full consciousness of their limitations because the goal of avoiding all labels is not in practice attainable.

6 / OBSERVATIONS ON THE POLITICAL PARTIES

Human Kind
Cannot bear very much reality

T. S. ELIOT, *Burnt Norton*

THE DOUBTS THAT HAVE BEEN CAST on the left–right spectrum do not in themselves demonstrate that there is anything wrong with the alignment of politicians into Labour and Conservative groupings. The present two-party system simply assumes that the views of both voters and politicians can be broadly divided into two groups. The conventional representation of opinion within these two broad groupings along two straight lines which meet head-on in the middle could be dropped without affecting the working of the party system. Thus the minimum thesis of this book, which is directed against the left–right spectrum, does not involve any call for the realignment of parties. But the wider, and more controversial, thesis is that the grouping of the parties around class issues—left–right in the looser sense—also has a harmful impact on political life, which now outweighs any benefit it may once have brought.

The inner workings of the parties, their history and the background of M Ps and Ministers have been discussed in a series of standard studies such as R. Mackenzie's *British Political Parties*,[1] Samuel Beer's *Modern British Politics*, Peter Pulzer's *Political Representation* and J. Blondel's *Voters, Parties and Leaders* (Blondel's book is a particularly thoughtful and stimulating summary). These explain, among many other features, the growing preponderance of middle-class M Ps in the Parliamentary Labour Party and the influence of the public-school hierarchy among Conservatives, including the disproportionate representation of Etonians in Conservative Cabinets. They also bring out less well-known points, such as the different parts of the middle class from which the two parties draw their M Ps. Labour Members tend to be teachers and lecturers, journalists or lawyers. Conservatives have even more lawyers, but instead of teachers and journalists, have businessmen, farmers and ex-members of the armed forces. A more subtle point is that although there are more businessmen than any other group among Conservative M Ps, these are mostly from the smaller firms or from the world of finance. Modern large-scale industry—which is supposed to be the key to the British economy—is virtually unrepresented.

Instead of enlarging on these matters, which are already well documented, I propose to devote this chapter to some miscellaneous reflections of my own on the party struggle in Britain today. Not all these necessarily reflect the left–right division. Some reflect the two-party basis of the system, some the personalities of the present leaders and some the technology of modern mass politics. The last few pages are devoted to a few thoughts on the Conservative Party, which presents many intriguing features, but is less transparent than Labour and therefore receives less than its due share of attention.

Among the biggest distortions brought about by the Labour–Conservative dialogue is that it exaggerates some conflicts but suppresses altogether other issues which the two front benches find convenient to keep out of the political arena. There are perhaps three or four reasons why so many of the major arguments of the day are put into quarantine. First, as they cut across party lines, there is the fear that they will cause 'splits'—or, if this is avoided, will not link up with the kind of issue on which the parties are accustomed to rally their supporters and harass the enemy. Secondly, the views of both front benches—say on certain matters of crime and punishment, education or the principles of tolerance and free speech—may be ahead of, or different from, majority opinion in the country; and there is no desire to emphasise this fact. Thirdly, certain sensitive issues of foreign and economic policy are not discussed by mutual consent for fear of embarrassing the authorities in international discussions or in the foreign exchange market. The tacit understanding is that the Government front bench would perform the same service if it became the Opposition. A fourth reason, on a very different plane, is a fear that certain issues will prove too technical and boring for much of the House of Commons, let alone for those who may read the debates in the newspapers. The common element which enters into several of the above reasons is the fear of the unknown and the unfamiliar.

This mixture of good, bad and doubtful considerations leads to an unhealthily great divide between what politicians think privately and what they believe it necessary to say in public. This caution is altogether excessive. Realistic admissions of private thoughts—for example when they emerge in unscripted interviews —very rarely do the harm that Civil Servants and Party bureaucrats suppose. The attitude of 'You can't say these things publicly' (e.g. the truth about the Commonwealth) is one of the main reasons for the widespread contempt for politicians, Parliament and the whole formal apparatus of public life.

The dichotomy between private and public utterances undermines the quality of political thought itself. So much of the professional time of politicians, officials and others is devoted to preparing public statements, or to the enunciation of prepared positions at formal confrontations, that this takes up most of their energy, leaving little time to work out what their true beliefs really are. The result is that when opportunities for frank private speaking arise, off-the-cuff pieces of cynicism too easily do duty for thought.

The suppression of public political debate on key issues also does more than anything else to strengthen the hand of the permanent Civil Service. This is not always harmful, as officials are often more conscious of policy problems than politicians, and less interested in purely public relations devices which leave basic problems untouched. Nevertheless the Civil Service, like most large institutions, is slow to change its established positions, and rarely does so without a great deal of prodding.

A debate between outside experts can sometimes be helpful, but cannot be relied upon to influence policy except after a harmful delay. Successive Governments refused to join the movement for European unity, when Britain would have been welcomed on its own terms; each successive step towards the Common Market came just that bit too late to succeed. If outside experts disagree with official policy, they best stand a chance of influencing it if they can bring their dissent into the political arena.

The situation has changed slightly in this respect since the late 1950s and early 1960s. One party had then been in power for a very long time and its tenure of office seemed almost part of the order of things. This near-monopoly situation had many unfortunate features, but it did provide a more fertile atmosphere for specialised discussion, unconnected with the party battle; such discussion did ultimately percolate to where the decisions were made, however belatedly. The early arguments on sterling, stop-go and growth were all of this kind. Although the Labour Party naturally cited the critics when it suited it, the main debate was outside the party framework; and so too were some of the initial acts of policy, such as the setting up of NEDC, and the new emphasis after about 1960 on measures to improve Britain's economic structure, such as industrial training, the new approach to the nationalised industries, the longer-term planning of Government expenditure and the use of economic regulators between Budgets.[2]

With the distintegration of the Macmillan Administration in 1962–3, this situation ceased to apply; as Ronald Butt remarks, the economy quickly came back into politics[3]—and indeed has never since left it. The result of the 1966 election, which gave Labour a secure majority, did not reduce the party political flavour of policy discussion. Election campaigns have become continuous, without the long lulls that took place in the Macmillan–Gaitskell era.

Partly as a result, ritual battles, which do not reflect real policy issues, grow forever fiercer. The party that happens to be in Opposition mounts more and more violent attacks on the other party on non-issues such as 'the high cost of living.' Opposition spokesmen attack with every show of fury Government policy on consensus subjects such as regional policy or official export promotion, which are developments by their own former Civil Servants of policies which they themselves began as Ministers, and which overlap by a factor of 90 per cent the activities they would be carrying out if they were still in office.

It may be argued that on such issues the Opposition spokesmen are acting like barristers in a court of law, who perform a useful function irrespective of their personal views on their briefs. Indeed positive harm might result if the Opposition passively accepted a certain degree of inflation, or rising unemployment, because of an overhonest recognition that it could not do better itself. (This incapacity may result either from the facts of the situation, or from a joint acceptance by Government and Opposition of certain restraints on policy.)

The intrusion of politics into specialised discussion is thus far from being an unmixed curse. Mr Heath was once reported to have offered to take unemployment out of party debate, if the Labour Party would do the same. Whether or not this offer was ever made, it is extremely fortunate that it was never taken up. For without the apparently cynical changing of sides when parties cross the floor, there would be no way in which the entirely legitimate dissatisfaction with the ever greater heights that unemployment has reached in each successive 'stop' period could make itself felt. Left to the pseudo-expert discussion of the Whitehall, City, CBI and TUC establishments, the intellectually unsound consensus that high unemployment is necessary for 'economic health' could all too easily have reigned triumphant, and the still small voice of academic or journalistic dissent would command no more attention than the discontent of those who had the misfortune to be out of work.

The danger of the barrister-like approach is that many of the participants in the end believe their own briefs. (It would not be a service to those concerned to name the front-benchers who are most free of this failing.) The most notable examples of the tendency to believe sincerely that their policies are 'utterly different' from those of the other side are the two Party Leaders themselves. It is almost certain that Mr Wilson really thought that his approach to the Common Market in 1967 diverged completely from Mr Heath's earlier attempt, and even possible that he thought his 'shake-out' of July 1966 was not comparable to Selwyn Lloyd's. Mr Heath for his part never seemed to appreciate that the small print of the National Plan—and indeed many of the other policies of the Department of Economic Affairs—were identical with what he had previously been promulgating himself at the Board of Trade.

The harm done by this top-level credulity is that party leaders do not learn from each other's mistakes, and the nation has to suffer the same policy errors repeatedly. Having persuaded the Conservatives that it was possible to enter the Common Market with the aid of the Five and without a political settlement with France, the Foreign Office then succeeded in selling the very same piece of wishful thinking all over again to Labour. One shudders to think of the frustration and disappointment when the Conservatives next come to office if those in the Party who talk most of a 'war on waste' in Whitehall, with the aid of computers and fashionable transatlantic slogans, do not take the trouble to find out what is already happening there.

A more serious result of the way in which the political game is played in Britain is that it seems to involve pretending that the nation is in a disastrous state whenever the other side is in office. This happens to a greater degree than in most other countries. Here is one of the origins of the national passion for self-denigration which never ceases to amaze foreigners. Politicians hardly ever admit that anything worth while may be going on in any home Department when the other party is in power. Although the real issues are avoided, the most hysterical pronouncements are in order about the state of the nation or its economy.

This combination of shadow-boxing and blanket denigration is closely connected with both the two-party system and the union of legislative and executive power in the House of Commons. Nevertheless I have the impression that these defects have worsened in the last few years. One has only to compare the Wilson Government's trumpeting of the inherited deficit in 1964 with the conduct in 1951 of the Churchill Government, which also inherited a severe payments deficit and faced a precarious Parliamentary majority. There may be something in the nature of present-day politics which puts scepticism, detachment or generosity of spirit at a discount in those who aspire to the topmost positions.

Another feature of the Labour–Conservative battle is that the difference between the two parties at any one time is a tiny fraction of the difference that exists between one party's policy today and that same party's policy a few years previously. This will always be the case if a sufficiently long period is taken. It is not surprising that Mr Heath's policy should differ less from Mr Wilson's than from the Duke of Wellington's. But the observation now applies over astonishingly short periods.

In 1967 the difference between official Labour and Conservative attitudes to the Common Market was minute. Both parties passionately wanted to join on any remotely respectable terms. The difference between Labour's 1967 attitudes and its coolness as recently as the 1966 General Election was much bigger than the inter-party gap. Even on the Conservative side there was a very large gulf between the whole-hearted commitment of 1967 and the strict conditions inserted in the 1961 application to meet party anxieties. If a ten-year comparison is made with the time when the majority of Conservatives insistently put the Commonwealth first, the change in opinion amounts to a policy revolution far, far greater than the gap that has ever existed between the two parties on this issue at any one date.

There have been just as large shifts in shorter periods in economic policy. At the time of the 1964 election, both parties were committed to acting directly on the balance of payments to prevent another economic 'stop.' (The import surcharge was devised under the Conservatives and implemented by Labour.) By the summer of 1966, the two front benches had retreated to the earlier Conservative policy of relying mainly on internal deflation to correct the balance of payments. The policy shift (or regression as some would call it) in less than two years was greater than the marginal difference between the two parties, who were basically agreed in both the years in question. The parties moved together even in their attitudes to controls and economic planning. The revulsion against physical controls in favour of overall financial management started under the post-war Labour Government at the end of the 1940s, before the Conservatives returned to office. Later on it was the Conservatives who took up 'indicative planning' and incomes policy in the early 1960s, both of which became gospel for the Labour Government of 1964.

A characteristic common to both of the present Party Leaders is that they tend to operate either with highly generalised slogans such as 'opportunity' or 'fairness,' or in terms of administrative details. Neither is at all interested in the intermediate ground of general ideas on policy, which are not slogans and can be stated with some rigour and logic, such as a properly argued belief in the market or John Strachey's pre-war Marxism. If the two parties had more interest in political ideas, the party argument could be at the same time more penetrating and more responsible. The two sides would be able to accept in a relaxed way, and without embarrassment, that their real differences were in attitudes to society and that these differences (which are immediately apparent to anyone who attends social gathering in both Labour and Conservative circles) far transcend the relatively minor divergencies within the practical range of policy choice. If the two parties were less afraid of being openly associated with different sets of values and different interest groups, there would be less need to pretend that the country is in a calamitous state whenever the wrong side is in power.

This reluctance to engage in general argument, combined with the issuing of shopping-lists of unrelated policy points, has its roots in the two-party system and the mass electorate. Indeed it is a characteristic feature of duopoly in a market characterised by imperfect information.[4] (Two rival department stores are more likely to be adjacent to each other in the High Street, rather than at opposite ends; and they are likely to copy each other's best-selling lines.)

Two other characteristics of British politics today are on the surface contradictory, but in fact blend all too well. One is the much-remarked slavery to public opinion polls. Majority views as revealed by the polls are regarded not merely as a constraint on policies, but as a source of policies, and even as a justification for them. The present Prime Minister has sometimes pointed to the polls—not merely the party preferences shown, but the answers given on specific issues—as proof of the rightness of his actions. The tendency is for policies to be marketed in closely resembling packages, in combinations revealed by market research—another duopoly feature.

In apparent conflict is the widespread view that unpopular and unpleasant policies must be good for the country. Selwyn Lloyd exclaimed, in July 1961, that he must be the most unpopular man in the country, as if this proved that his squeeze was appropriate. Mr Wilson frequently stressed how (having just won an election after a promise of no major increase in taxes) he did not hesitate to take unpopular economic measures irrespective of political consequences. Political commentators duly gave the Government credit for courage in carrying out such policies.

The paradox is not as great as it seems. Opinion surveys show that the majority of the electorate often themselves seem to think that policies which hurt are *ipso facto* beneficial. Support for such measures wears off after a time, as people become tired with the reality, as distinct from the idea, of sacrifice. Nevertheless most voters' own diagnosis of the country's ills is very much in terms of sin and punishment. They are, they believe, not working hard enough and are earning too much money. There is an under-lying belief that prosperity or easy times are sinful and must eventually be paid for.

The marketing of immediately popular policies, interspersed with painful purges, leaves no room for *rational* policies of long-term hedonism, going beyond what most voters would have been able to imagine for themselves. Unfortunately, the psychology of both the individuals who lead the two main parties reflects and contributes towards the vogue for pseudo-toughness. The worst that either Mr Wilson or Mr Heath can say about a proposal is that it is 'the easy way out'—which does not prevent it from being adopted in the end, in Mr Wilson's case anyway. Mr Heath has stressed that he believes in doing things the hard way, not the easy way, a view that comes close to a definition of the irrational in conduct.

So far this chapter has been concerned with the style of the political struggle and the reactions of the two main parties to changing events. It should, however, never be forgotten that the two main parties exist only partly to express opinions and attitudes. They are differentiated mainly by their class images and by the different material interest groups which look to them for support. The main issues which are relevant to interest groups are who should get how much of the cake. The nature of the interests served is thus often a better guide to politicians' attitudes than professed ideology. The pronounced official Conservative em-phasis on a competitive society did not prevent a group of London Conservative MPs from championing the taxis against the mini-cabs; nor has it prevented the Party from becoming even more protectionist in its agricultural policy.

Few people, when considering their own material interests, are very enlightened or inclined to take a long view. This near-sighted materialism is pardonable, when one remembers that it is only since the last war that most people have made anything more than a bare living; and a relatively minor financial buffeting would be sufficient to deprive many of the middle class, let alone the workers, of the not very extravagant comforts so arrogantly described as affluence.

It is, however, important to distinguish between materialism, even near-sighted materialism, and producer interest groups. There is an inherent bias in almost all political societies in favour of producers at the expense of consumers. This is because the benefits of any restrictionist measures are highly concentrated among a limited number of organised groups, whether coal-miners or the City of London, while their disadvantages are thinly spread among the whole population. Thus in any particular case the producers have much more at stake than the consumers and more incentive to exert political pressure, quite apart from the fact that they are better organised for the purpose. Producer interests are also helped, relative to consumers', because, as Professor Harry Johnson has pointed out,[5] they are geographically concentrated, and parliamentary representation is based on residence.

One of the worst mistakes of would-be realist political writers is to identify the general welfare with the sum of the welfare of interest groups. The precise opposite is closer to the truth; the general welfare is more nearly represented by consumer interests. This would still be so if every consumer were also a producer. If restrictive measures were taken to help every producer interest to the same extent, the gains would cancel each other out; but as the real national income would be depressed, all concerned would suffer. They would therefore be better off if the game had never started. The validity of this last conclusion is impaired in practice because some producers, such as miners and farmers, have greater power of leverage than others as a result of their above-average geographical concentration, which gives them disproportionate influence in one or other of the political parties.

Even more depressing is the fact that pressure groups are not always guided by a rational assessment of their own self-interest, but often have mistaken stereotyped notions of where it lies. These stereotypes are at work even among the most expensively educated groups. It is, for example, at least arguable that many City institutions would gain from a more rapidly expanding economy and one in which the City was freed from the network of capital and exchange restrictions. This might have happened if the sterling exchange rate had been changed earlier, and perhaps allowed to float. The unanimity and emotion with which the opposing view was put forward by all those who spoke for the City was not based on a logical appraisal. On the contrary, the men concerned were behaving like a herd showing loyalty to their leader—the Bank of England, whose views were taken on trust. However much one tries to avoid making facile gibes at the public-school ethos, one was conscious of it oozing out of every nook and cranny of the City whenever the exchange rate was mentioned in the three years from 1964 to 1967.

An even more blatant example was the attitude of industrialists —or at least their official leaders—after devaluation came. Whatever its other merits or defects, devaluation is almost invariably good for profits. Yet the CBI, and even some working industrialists, appeared to dispute this and spoke as if a blow had been struck at their financial prospects. Part of the explanation lies in sheer misunderstanding and the lack of adequate briefing. But even more important was the way in which so many industrialists, concerned to hold respectable views at all costs, had been brainwashed by the political and financial establishments into thinking that devaluation would be a national disaster.

The last few pages present, of course, a one-sided picture. Despite all the obstacles, the coal-mines are being run down, uneconomic railway branch lines have been cut, tariffs have been reduced and the pound has been devalued (however belatedly). There are clearly other forces at work (some of which can be summarised as 'money running out of the till') working against the interest groups and in favour of change. There is unfortunately no general theory to determine the point at which these opposing forces balance.

In many ways, British politics would be healthier if the division between the two main parties were more overtly materialistic. To the extent that the main parties adopt comprehensive policies going beyond the basic cake-dividing issues, important sections of opinion are under-represented in Parliament; in particular non-egalitarian middle-class voters of intellectually radical, or humanitarian, views, and working-class voters of a reactionary and xenophobic frame of mind. (So too are the many xenophobic members of the middle class whose views go beyond anything found among the Parliamentary Tory Right.) In my experience many of the more humane or radical middle-class voters regard non-class issues as being in a different compartment from the Labour–Conservative battle. They are often unaware of the very limited support that exists for their views even among the most 'advanced' Conservative leaders; and if they are aware of it, do not think it matters.

It may be argued that the absence of the Freudian free-thinker who happens to be a capitalist, or the 'bash-Nasser' proletarian, from the House of Commons does not matter in practice, as the component parts of these attitudes are already well enough represented. It is not easy to say whether this is a satisfactory substitute or not. MPs cannot be divided up into parcels of separate policy attitudes. The absence of certain combinations of attitudes among the main sections of Parliamentary opinion does probably have an influence on both Government and Opposition policy. One cannot help feeling that political life would be healthier if it were more broadly representative of the range of views in the country. This is not just a plea for more middle-class MPs of fashionably enlightened views. Some writers such as Ronald Butt would argue that there are enough of them already there in the 1964 and 1966 intake disguised as Labour MPs. If this is so, is it really a good thing that they should have to wear the disguise? There is an equally good case for having the reactionary egalitarians represented more nearly in proportion to their real strength.

Cynics often say that politicians are more enlightened in opposition than in power. With the Conservatives it is the other way round. They seem incapable of being enlightened in opposition, when all their most atavistic instincts take over: determination to hang on to the relics of empire, belief in the health-giving effects of unemployment, subservience to every industrial lobby. Worst of all is an inability to differentiate between slogans and coherent policies. This inability ultimately reflects the gap between the world of the Civil Servant and academic, and that of Conservative politicians, a gap that is even greater than in the case of their Labour counterparts. The differences between the middle-class Labour and middle-class Conservative MPs, mentioned at the beginning of the chapter, are relevant here. It is perhaps because of this greater gap that Conservative Ministers are more inclined, especially in home policy, to accept Civil Service advice.

With certain exceptions, such as Enoch Powell, the Conservatives are deeply ill at ease in Opposition; their leaders are temperamentally unsuited to it, and the party has little sense of the constructive opportunities, the excitement and the joy to be had in the role. None of this is surprising as it has not only been in power most of the time, but is traditionally the party of authority and the state, not of rebellion and dissent.

To the outside observer the Conservative Opposition has presented a very curious spectacle since 1964. It attacked the Government fiercely on decisions, such as the withdrawal from Britain's world power role, which had the support of many informed people, including some in business and finance, who normally voted Conservative. On the other hand, it hesitated to attack the Government even where a strong onslaught could have been made which would have unified all non-socialists and embarrassed some of the more thoughtful Labour supporters. There was no real attack, for example, on the 1966 travel restrictions or the surcharge on surtax, both economically irrelevant appeals to class prejudice.

It would be an exaggeration to say that the only ideas that the Conservatives were prepared to discuss aloud after the 1966 election were played-back slogans from the early 1950s, calling for lower Government spending and reduced taxes, without saying how except by sacking Civil Servants. The Party's proposals for trade union reform, industrial re-training and more selective social services were well worth putting forward, even though they were neither as revolutionary, nor as different from what Labour was likely to do, as was claimed. But too much that is interesting is either concealed from the public view or confined to subtle nuances which no outsider is going to bother to notice. Fear of unfavourable headlines resulting from any public discussion far outweigh any fear of losing support through dullness, or apparent irrelevance to the issues of the day.

The absence of serious Opposition when Labour is in power leaves a great gap in political life. The Conservatives seem content to rely on disillusionment with Labour to bring them back to office; this is at least a less risky formula than serious political discussion. The really extraordinary aspect, however, of the present leadership of the Conservatives has been its hostility to the use of the price mechanism and the profit-motive. In the post-devaluation argument the parties seemed to have reversed their accepted roles. Exchange-rate adjustments work by making exports cheaper to foreigners, or more profitable to British producers, or both. They are thus an alternative, not only to relying solely on deflation, but also to physical controls. Yet in the end Labour settled for devaluation, while the Conservatives came out with a misconceived root-and-branch opposition to it.

The implication of Conservative speeches, both before and after devaluation, was that any sacrifice of employment and production, any resort to the devices of a siege economy (to which their Party was supposed to be vehemently opposed), indeed any sacrifice whatever, was to be preferred to a change in the parity. Indeed the Conservatives found themselves in a position, before November 1967, where they could not logically attack restrictions on overseas investment or travel, loyalty rebates for nationalised steel, or even wage and price controls. For these were all back-door methods of discouraging imports or making exports more competitive; and indeed Conservative opposition on these matters was suitably tepid when it existed at all.

The attitude of being 'totally opposed' to devaluation was far from necessary for tactical or political reasons. With a little imagination it would have been so easy to say that devaluation would not have been necessary if the economy had been managed properly, and to concentrate the attack on the alleged mismanagement that made it appropriate, rather than the act itself. This was the line taken by Mr Maudling, the only Conservative frontbencher with first-hand top-level knowledge of these matters. In political terms the Opposition attitude was based on an innocent belief that the piety of the establishment towards the pound was deeply shared by the general public. By the next election public opinion will be influenced by the general prosperity of the country, living standards and employment. If from this point of view devaluation seems to have worked, there will be few converts to Conservatism on the grounds of supposed national dishonour.

Misguided tactics were, I believe, only part of the picture. A good many Conservatives were in fact shocked at the idea that anyone connected with their party should ever countenance moving the exchange rate. This came out at a Conservative Economic Conference on 20 July 1967, to which outside experts were invited, and where—to the horror of the leadership—the morning's discussion moved in favour of devaluation and floating rates. The idea that the party that was supposed to stand for a market economy should prefer a price mechanism adjustment to import controls, backdoor export subsidies, travel restrictions and all the other paraphernalia of a siege economy, was regarded as too horrible to contemplate. One speaker got up to protest that the conference was 'like a *Tribune* meeting,' which itself showed how inapplicable the conventional political spectrum had become.

It is regrettable but not surprising that on all the key issues of the recent past outside the normal domestic political argument such as devaluation, Vietnam, or East of Suez, the Conservative front bench should have come down on the anti-radical side. What was much more open to objection was the attempt to stifle criticism—at times even criticism of the Labour Government—from among the Conservative ranks. There was, for example, the ukase imposed by Mr Heath, in July 1967, against any discussion of devaluation or floating rates by Conservative back-benchers, which was accepted in docile fashion. Then again in his out-and-out endorsement in early 1968 of the American line on Vietnam—which might have embarrassed President Johnson himself by its unreserved quality—Mr Heath insisted that he was speaking 'on behalf of the whole of the Tory Party.' It is enough that Ministers should be bound to accept the myth of joint Cabinet responsibility. There is no need to pretend that the Shadow Cabinet is a real Cabinet and apply the same rules to it. Those involved are in one sense taking themselves and their role absurdly over-seriously. But their real duty of stimulating critical discussion is neglected for the sake of this Shadow role. Even if the myth of the Shadow Cabinet has to be accepted, back-benchers on both sides provide the last refuge for free-ranging critical discussion. It had always been the tradition that Opposition back-benchers could put forward heretical ideas without committing their Party officially; unfortunately this tradition has been increasingly challenged inside the Conservative Party.

These autocratic tendencies may have been reinforced by personal factors, but their roots go back a long way in Conservative tradition. There are two alternative defences of inequality and private ownership against socialist criticism, the liberal capitalist defence, and an answer in terms of the need for hierarchy and order. Most Tory thinkers have adopted the second alternative. It is striking how many Conservatives go out of their way to assert a positive belief in the class system, by which they mean something more than division between rich and poor, or more and less influential, which exists in all Western societies. One way in which this is expressed is an emphasis on the 'rulers versus the ruled.' The attitude has the virtue of honesty; it involves an acceptance and defence of views which seem like socialist parodies. Of course such attitudes are too unfashionable to be expressed in public by Conservative politicians; but they can often be heard in private and they form the staple diet of self-consciously right-wing journalism.

This attitude stands in the starkest possible contrast to that of the enthusiasts for competitive free enterprise (represented, for example, by the Institute of Economic Affairs) who see in the market mechanism a way of widening the individual's area of decision-making, and generally replacing status by contractual relations. The economically libertarian views of a Hayek or a Milton Friedman, or even of the non-socialist Keynesians, form no part of the English intellectual Conservative tradition, which is not the opposite of socialism, but something different.

This tradition does have related to it a literature of great subtlety and quality. The key to this body of thought is that it originated as a defence against liberalism rather than socialism. It emphasises the importance of habit and unconscious forces, and the limitations of reason in politics. The key figures include Burke, Oakeshott, R. J. White, the Hogg of *The Case for Conservatism* and J. L. Talmon. But it is just as strongly represented among literary figures from Coleridge to Eliot (and Yeats in some of his moods). As not all these figures identified themselves with a political party, it might be tempting to regard their outlook as conservative with a small 'c'. Certainly most of them would regard with contempt (or at most as a disagreeable necessity) the wholesale adoption of the heresy of progress by recent Conservative leaders. On the other hand it is to this tradition that many thoughtful Conservatives with a capital 'C' have turned when they reflected on their fundamental beliefs, certainly far more frequently than to any liberal apologetics in favour of the market place.

This *intellectual conservatism* is a uniquely English growth. Although many of those who have contributed to it have not been English at all, and it draws upon European writers—above all Dostoevsky—the blend is not available elsewhere. In this it differs from socialism and egalitarianism which, for all the endearingly British features of the Labour Party, are international. Judged by logical coherence or by its ethical concepts, the conservative tradition is inferior to the harder, but also more humanitarian, empirical school going from Locke, via Bentham and Mill, to

Russell and Keynes. Yet its contribution to an understanding of human behaviour and history is probably greater than that of most schools of socialist and liberal writing.

One of the most intellectually attractive aspects of this kind of traditional Conservatism is its scepticism about the ability of governments, at least non-totalitarian governments, to bring about fundamental and quick changes in human society. Unfortunately, while the authoritarian element in traditional Conservatism remains very much in evidence, this sceptical element is today at a discount. It is still represented in different ways, but the dominant strain in the party is insistent that a Conservative Government will transform British society and remove the painful problems of choice which have plagued British Governments since the end of the war. The spark of scepticism that humanised Conservative leaders from Disraeli to Macmillan seems to have gone, and this is a real loss to contemporary politics.

7 / THE DILEMMA OF CHOICE

Freude, schöner Götterfunken,
Tochter aus Elysium.

SCHILLER, *An die Freude*

Thou radiance sprung from the gods:
Thou daughter of Elysium, Joy.

(The reference is generally taken to be freedom, not joy. The substitution
was made for reasons of political discretion.)

E

THIS CHAPTER IS RATHER MORE PERSONAL than the rest of
the essay. It is written because of a belief that my own inability
to choose between the two main parties may raise issues of more
general interest.

My main difficulty in choosing between the two very broad
coalitions that make up the two political parties is that the side I
should like to be on is that of liberalism, on the liberal versus
authoritarian dimension described in Chapter 5. This makes
choice extremely difficult when the two main parties are authoritarian in philosophy and tradition. The Conservatives have traditionally been the party of authority—of Church, Crown, the
aristocracy, and the Armed Services—while Labour's whole
political vocabulary puts the stress on the community against the
individual. Although the two traditions are often played down for
electoral reasons, they are still very much alive and frequently
come to the surface.

The dilemma of the liberal is that while the Conservatives now
use the language of individual freedom, they apply this only—
if at all—to domestic economic questions. They are the less
libertarian of the two parties—despite individual exceptions—
on all matters of personal and social conduct, and are much the
more hawk-like in their attitude to 'foreign affairs.' Labour, on
the other hand, has liberal instincts on foreign affairs and personal conduct, but is perversely blind to the claims of economic
liberty, which is distrusted as a capitalist rationalisation.

Socialists in the literary and theatrical world, who rightly leap
in to protest when civil liberties or freedom of expression are
threatened, usually want to increase the economic role of the

State. Professor Tom Wilson has pointed to the inherent ambiguity of this position, as the 'end of private enterprise, and still more the end of free markets, would bring every form of artistic expression under state control.'[1] The treatment that Russian writers have recently experienced is just one unpleasant reminder of this fact. As Mr Grimond remarked about the row over Lord Chandos's refusal to allow the National Theatre to produce a play he considered offensive: 'It is no good constantly clamouring for state intervention all over the place, and then complaining when the State in intervening lives up to its inherent nature and purpose.'[2]

One example of this blindness on the left to the economic aspects of freedom was the readiness of the Labour Government to impose a travel allowance which virtually confined Britons to this country, except for a two weeks' cheese-paring vacation, as a cheap political gesture. Yet one of the severest restrictions it is possible for Governments to impose on personal liberty in time of peace was greeted with hardly a word of protest from all Labour's intellectual camp-followers.

The inconsistency in attitudes towards freedom is as great among Conservatives—I think greater because they go out of their way to identify themselves with the cause of the individual hit by state restrictions. In a recent debate on the Liberties of the Subject, Sir Dingle Foot recalled that when a Labour Member introduced in 1954 a Bill to prevent deportations from, or rustication in, any British Colony without a preceding trial, it received no Tory support at all. During the Kenya emergency, when thousands of men and women were detained for two and a half years without trial, scarcely a week passed without some form of protest from Labour benches, but there was not a single note of protest from anywhere on the Conservative side.[3] On a very different libertarian issue, a Bill introduced in 1962 to abolish the Lord Chamberlain's censorship of stage plays was defeated by 134 to 77 votes. Of the 77 two were Conservatives. It took a Labour House of Commons to give such a Bill an unopposed Second Reading in 1968.

The 1967 Tory Conference carried by an overwhelming majority an extreme resolution disapproving 'any move towards a more permissive attitude to the so-called soft drugs.' It disapproved not merely of legalisation, but of any re-examination of the present law, for which eminent medical experts have asked. In a speech in the House of Commons Mr Quintin Hogg expressed the charitable Christian wish that addicts of hashish and marijuana would be pursued 'with the utmost severity the law allows. I hope that they find themselves in the Old Bailey and, however distinguished their positions in the Top Ten, that they will be treated as criminals deserve to be treated.'⁴ In his subsequent speech to the Tory Conference, which received a standing ovation, he said it was a 'grave error' for the Editor of *The Times* even to publish the advertisement asking for the legalisation of cannabis, calling it 'a heavy responsibility which the new Editor will have to bear for the rest of his professional life.'⁵

It is, moreover, difficult to escape from the identification of the Tory Party with the public-school culture. According to a leading authority, Dr Royston Lambert, the distinguishing feature of the public schools still is that they 'attempt a more complete control over their pupils' lives and minds' than other schools, even other boarding schools. This extends to their 'moral values and beliefs, their intimate relationships and social reactions, their tastes, their access to outside society and its expressions. Access to shops, cinema, coffee bars, books, television and—of course—the opposite sex is minutely prescribed in the light of the schools' values.' The public-schoolboy has 'to live without privacy under the savage scrutiny of an all-male society' and to conceal many kinds of emotion.⁶

It may be that Dr Lambert has underestimated the degree to which some public schools have been liberalised—this is always claimed in every generation. But it is difficult to deny that there is still a powerful tendency in the direction he describes. Making the maximum allowance for the special position of minors, the values of the public school are at the opposite pole from those of John Stuart Mill's *On Liberty*, which argues that individuals should be free to lead their own lives and form their own beliefs provided they do not harm others.

Two important points follow in a political context. The liberal cannot conceivably associate himself with the case for compulsory state education, or even of tax or other laws which impose artificial obstacles to independent education. To do so would be to abandon all belief in diversity, experiment and parents' rights in favour, not even of equality, but of social uniformity. (Equality could be secured by giving every parent education vouchers to be spent at a school of his choice, but forbidding him to supplement them with his own money. I would regard the latter restraint as intolerable. I only mention the possibility to show that even extreme egalitarianism does not imply universal state education.) On the other hand it is difficult for a liberal to feel much enthusiasm for a freedom which in practice encourages schools which put a special stress on conformity. Both sides of conventional argument are at heart illiberal.

The second interesting point is the close resemblance of public-school ideals to the traditional values of the Labour Party, especially of its trade union section. The stress on services to the community, team spirit, and the subordination of self-interest are collectivist values they share in common. They are at the opposite pole from the liberal capitalist belief in enlightened self-interest. The similarity between a socialist society and a good public school was one of Hugh Dalton's favourite themes.

Fortunately for the cause of freedom, the two parties are not entirely monolithic. There are Conservatives, such as Sir Edward Boyle, who take their party's libertarian slogans seriously in social behaviour as well as in economic policy, and no more wish to see 'that dangerous abstraction society attempting to prescribe ethical standards' than plan in detail what should be produced.[7] Sir Edward has done well to protest against the use of the word 'permissive' as a pejorative synonym for 'free.'

Unfortunately, Sir Edward's views are far from characteristic of his colleagues. It is worth noting that Mr St John Stevas, who is regarded as on the liberal wing of the Tory Party, said, in the Liberties of the Subject Debate, that 'perhaps permissiveness has gone far enough' and that we were 'in danger of destroying the moral consensus on which our society is based.' The fact is that the underlying beliefs of both parties lean towards authority rather than the individual.

The divorce between economic and other kinds of liberalism is a relatively recent phenomenon. Professor Wilson recalls how in the nineteenth century 'a gradual removal of restrictions on trade' went together 'with a wider freedom under the law to express one's views and shape one's own moral and religious life.' In modern times, the same forces that are fighting to reduce centralised economic planning in Communist countries are also associated with a movement towards freedom in wider spheres, even though the two movements often get out of phase.

Some Socialists have the greatest difficulty in accepting that the 'bourgeois liberal' idea of freedom is anything but a piece of hypocrisy. The more extreme form of hostility is to deny that a dweller in a Birmingham slum in the golden age of nineteenth-century Liberalism, or an Egyptian peasant today, can in any real sense be said to be 'free' irrespective of his political rights. Sir Isaiah Berlin has dealt with this once and for all, pointing out that 'freedom is not the mere absence of frustration of whatever kind; this would inflate the meaning of the word until it meant too much or too little.'[8] There are situations where bread, or protection against disease, may be more important than freedom. But 'liberty is liberty, not equality or fairness or justice or human happiness or a quiet conscience.' It is not the only value; there are occasions when others may take precedence, but it only confuses the issue to broaden the concept of freedom to take in all the others. Freedom for an Egyptian peasant *is* the same as freedom for an Oxford don, even though it is less important to him. The relevance of modern technology and general affluence is that, as other needs are satisfied, the debate over the area of personal freedom becomes important to the whole population and not only to the upper and middle classes. The reason for concentrating on personal freedom in this chapter is that a choice between the two parties is more difficult from the standpoint of this value than of any other.

A more deep-seated difficulty is the bias of even Gaitskellite Labour thinkers in favour of State activity and expenditure. Yet, *other things being equal*, preference for public expenditure over allowing individuals to spend their own money is a sign of paternalist rather than liberal leanings because it implies that individuals cannot be trusted to spend their money in their own way. This is so, even though many people do not realise the paternalist implications. There are non-paternalist reasons for favouring state expenditure. It may be advocated as a method of income redistribution. The test is whether the protagonists of the public sector would still prefer a high level of state expenditure, if income redistribution could be brought about more directly, through say a system of positive and negative income tax.

Another non-paternalist reason for high state spending is the belief that the most important ingredients in a civilised standard of living—such as good schools, parks or roads—happen to be in the state sector. The acid test of paternalism here is whether a positive virtue is seen in the state taking the decisions in these spheres out of private hands, or whether it is simply believed that private decisions in these areas are either not technically feasible at all, or feasible only at too great a cost in inequality. In the latter case there would be a choice to make. It is I think fair to say that very few Labour thinkers lose much sleep over these questions, and anyone who raises them is likely to be treated as showing the cloven hoof. Among Labour-sympathising economists there are few more abusive epithets than 'economic liberal.'

The Conservative–Socialist division, like similar polarisations in other countries, hides from public view the older and more fundamental argument between liberty and authority. This has for a long time been symbolised for me by two characters in Thomas Mann's *The Magic Mountain*, who battle for the mind of the young engineer Hans Castorp. One was Settembrini, a somewhat operatic Italian liberal who proclaims 'Democracy has no meaning whatever if not that of an individualistic corrective to state absolutism of every kind.' He favours both national self-determination and the abolition of war through international law. A passionate anti-ascetic (who lives in a garret) he loves 'form, beauty, freedom, gaiety, the enjoyment of life.' His more formidable antagonist is a Jesuit, Naphta, who believes in 'discipline, sacrifice, the renunciation of the ego, the curbing of the personality.' He is also a revolutionary socialist, who looks forward to a new authoritarian order to be achieved by the proletariat. Freedom, he believes is a pathetic bourgeois illusion. He despises the humanist philosophers whose aim was 'to make men grow old and happy, rich and comfortable.' He reveres physical suffering, war and corporal punishment, all fit chastisements for the corruption of the body. His favourite quotation is Gregory the Great's: 'Cursed be the man who holds back his sword from the shedding of blood.'

Mann is careful not to identify Naphta with mainstream Catholic orthodoxy. Owing to bad health he has never been admitted to the priesthood. Moreover, before the end of the novel his malignant views have overstepped the borderline of sanity.

Provoked by Settembrini he challenges him to a duel. Settembrini tries to reconcile honour with humanitarian principles by firing into the air. Shouting 'Coward!' Naphta shoots himself in the head. It is interesting that although Mann partially identifies himself with Settembrini, it is Naphta who wins the arguments.

Most people as they go about their business are, needless to say, remote from both characters. Yet they are of value as representatives of the two opposite poles between which positions have to be taken for the purposes of practical decision. If Mann had published his book later than 1924, he could have furnished Settembrini with more powerful arguments, as a result of the actual experiences of totalitarian systems such as those of Nazi Germany or Soviet Russia which tried to put Naphta's ideal of the complete subordination of the individual to the collective into practice. The interest of Naphta's tirades is that they bring out with a wealth of cogent detail that liberalism is not a middle way between conservatism and socialism, but at the opposite extreme. All the collectivist varieties of socialism, and the forms of conservatism which emphasise authority and obedience, have much more in common with each other than they have with systems of thought which attach a high value to individual freedom.

Naphta's form of anti-liberalism might seem too hysterical to be worth taking seriously. But if the mentally unbalanced elements and the Teutonic emotional charge are removed, some of the demands of his philosophy can be found in as civilised a writer as Eliot himself.[9] The latter's *Idea of a Christian Society* is to a large extent an attack on liberalism for destroying traditional social habits, 'licensing the opinions of the most foolish' and fostering the notion of 'getting on.' Eliot's 'Christian' alternative involves—in words reminiscent of Naphta in a more sober mood —'discipline, inconvenience and discomfort.' He believes that a people feels 'at least more dignified if its hero is the statesmen however unscrupulous, or the warrior however brutal, rather than the financier.' He criticises severely 'the organisation of society on the principle of private profit.' He insists that the pacifist repudiates an obligation towards society, 'and in so far as the society is a Christian society the obligation is so much the more serious.'[10] In his indictment of bourgeois liberalism Eliot quite naturally combines traditional conservative and semi-socialist elements.

There is, of course, a good deal of validity in some of Eliot's observations, for example when he remarks that 'in a negative liberal society you have no agreement as to there being any body of knowledge which any educated person should have acquired at any particular stage.'[11] A continuing tension between those who attach most weight to authority and those who put forward the claims of personal freedom is natural and healthy. A complete victory for either side is neither desirable nor possible.

Liberalism does indeed have one glaring gap as a political creed. Freedom has no positive content; it is up to the individual to make the best of his life if the pressures of authority are relaxed. This is perhaps why it can be celebrated best in music or lyrical poetry, or the two in combination, such as in the Ode to Joy at the end of the Ninth Symphony. A liberal is someone who responds neither to hierarchy nor to working-class solidarity, but to the trumpet call in the Second Act of *Fidelio* announcing the liberation of the prisoners. The question remains: what are the prisoners to do when they have been liberated and the orchestra has stopped playing? The liberal does not supply the answer. He refuses to play the role of archbishop. In his view there is plenty for the politician to do in his own field without solving the personal problems of individual life. The field of political action may be limited and negative; it is none the worse for that.

If this central void is admitted, it is easy to see why pure liberalism has never been for long a popular creed. The feeling of many people that they need to belong to something outside themselves is an excessively familiar truth; and liberalism, strictly interpreted, gives this feeling no outlet. Nationalism, which gives it at least a superficial outlet, has always proved to have far greater popular appeal. Recent evidence of this yearning to belong was given by the pride taken by even the most assimilated, sophisticated and pacific Jews in Israel's triumphs in the 1967 War, and their complete identification with Israel's case in the subsequent territorial disputes.

One thing seems highly likely. This is that people do not find straightforward hedonism a completely satisfactory way of occupying their time when they achieve reasonable prosperity and freedom from compulsion. This is equally true whether this hedonism takes the traditional form of the pursuit of the arts or the contemporary pursuit of sex, or both. It is easy to see why writers such as Pound, Eliot and Yeats should have turned with horror from liberal humanism to embrace a sterner and more aristocratic ideal; to ask as Yeats did in *Three Marching Songs*

> Where are the captains that
> govern mankind?
> What happens to a tree which has
> nothing within it?

Such writers sometimes mistook the nature of fascism, and did not realise that, so far from being a repudiation of mass culture in the interests of a classical ideal, it was itself the most vulgar of mass movements. The features of modern society that these writers found so sordid and *ersatz* were not due to liberalism alone, but reflected liberalism in a modern mass society. Still, this does not dispose of their arguments, as this is the only form of liberalism that is relevant in the twentieth century.[12]

Nevertheless in my mind the scales are decisively weighted against the anti-liberal school of writers when one observes the exponents of the ordered society in action: the hatred and jealousy of youth, the intolerance and hunt for scapegoats which came to the surface at the time of the trial of the Rolling Stones, the bizarre nightmare of the Greek Colonels, the rigid hierarchical disciplines of the army or the public schools. If Settembrini's vision leads in the last resort to *The Waste Land*, I would settle for that rather than for Naphta's authoritarian nightmare.

There is, moreover, a moral contradiction at the heart of the ordered society, as put forward by its many representatives in the British Conservative Party. A Tory from this stable is highly moral and censorious in relation to personal conduct; he will have no truck with cynicism, permissiveness or *laisser-faire* in relation to drug-taking or juvenile error. He is convinced that there are absolute rules of conduct to which individuals must be made to conform. Yet this is allied with a hard, cynical, *Realpolitik* view of foreign policy in which any form of moral ideal is scorned, and the concept of killing and wounding as an instrument of policy accepted. Even at home the exponent of traditional Conservatism often offers all the unpleasant features of a 'moral' view of society with its stress on discipline, conformism and punishment, but without the compensating dream of a better society held out by the puritan Socialist. There is a great deal of validity in Conservative scepticism about the possibilities of moral betterment; but this scepticism lacks the redeeming feature of toleration which ought to go with it, and to some extent did among the old Whigs.

I have no particular solution to the age-old problem of what is to take the place of war, or provide a substitute in a permissive society for the thrill of flaunting authority. If answers are reached, they are to be found in the writings of anthropologists and social psychologists; and a study of their writings to sort out the useful wheat from the Ph.D. chaff would be useful. Despite the massive infiltration of the pedant and the time-server and the more innocent searcher after academic posts, the development and *application* of the social sciences still seem to me the only way to improve the happiness of the race after material needs have been satisfied.

These difficulties, together with the fact that it is hard to attach strong class interests to the politics of freedom for more than brief historical periods, help to explain why neither of the major parties is a liberal one. It does not prove liberalism wrong or not worth propagating. It would, however, be unwise for the liberal to rely on the pure assertion of freedom as a value-judgment. He usually does better to supplement his basic position by careful statements of the specific disadvantages and absurdities of compulsion and the benefits of freedom in particular cases. Such arguments form the bulk of Mill's *On Liberty*. As Professor Wilson remarks, 'The sheer inefficiency of overextended government control is often the best defence of freedom.'

The difficulty of the present political line-up is that neither major party stands for the libertarian side of this argument. One cannot expect political parties facing each other across the floor of the House to embody in pure form the belief-systems of writers in their studies. But in the nineteenth-century House of Commons there was no doubt that, for all its imperfections and disparate elements, the Liberal Party—and even its Whig predecessor— was the natural place for anyone who wished to place the emphasis on freedom rather than authority. Such a person has today to decide between two main parties divided by attitudes to equality rather than liberty.

Relationships between views on different subjects do not have the authority of logic or mathematics. There are historical, sociological and cultural explanations why a bias towards economic freedom should be combined with an anti-permissive approach to social questions and relatively belligerent external attitudes among Conservatives—just as there are for the combination of state economic intervention, a bias towards freedom in personal behaviour and pacific external attitudes among the Labour Party. But these combinations are not part of the permanent order of things. At least as good a case can be made for putting together in Cobdenite fashion economic and personal freedom and non-intervention overseas. Indeed a political dialogue in terms of freedom versus order, or non-intervention versus more ambitious external objectives, may be more appropriate to an affluent society, in which status barriers have partially crumbled, than the present class-dominated alignments which have emerged from the first half of this century.

The present party alignment leaves no place for a present-day Cobden. There are Tory doves, but they are rarely heard in the House, where the main drift of Conservative criticism has been to oppose the British Government's (excessively slow and belated) withdrawal from its post-imperial role in Asia. Only one Conservative MP, Mr Bruce-Gardyne, abstained from voting for the Conservative Amendment on the latter issue in the 1967 Defence Debate. Iain Macleod once used the concept of a Conservative pacifist as a metaphor for the virtually impossible. This is precisely what is wrong with the Conservative Party. My complaint is not directed against the absence of a large number of Conservative MPs so unrealistic in their approach to peace that they would be against the use of military force in any circumstances. But a party that had a large Cobdenite element with a heavy bias in favour of 'peace and non-intervention' might be expected to have a small pacifist extreme; and the absence of the latter is symptomatic of the imbalance of views within the Party. This imbalance has shown itself on innumerable occasions: the overwhelming backing for Eden's Suez expedition, the lack of misgivings on the Tory benches when the Central African Federation was imposed in the face of clear native opposition, and the absence of protest by Conservative Members at the prolonged attempt to hold Cyprus down by military force. One can imagine a Labour Government perpetrating similar policies. What one cannot imagine is their being carried out without the strongest opposition from the Labour side of the House.

If politics were confined to narrowly economic issues, I would be prepared to settle without enthusiasm for the Conservative side. Even here, official Conservative policies are more retrograde than Labour's on a wide range of 'macroeconomic' policies. But on these it would be legitimate to argue from within. At heart the Conservatives have a limited view of the ends of economic activity and do not believe in the 'purposeful' direction of production towards the goods and services that happen to be in favour with the Government of the day. One would at least be free of the desire to favour some classes of output at the expense of others and to regard the test of profit as immoral, a view that is never far below the surface in the Labour Party, however alien it may be to individual Ministers. One would at least be free of the pseudo-egalitarianism of the travel allowance imposed in 1966— the type of argument that because 'you' can have an 'adequate' holiday for £50, this is all that should be allowed—as if how much I spend on holiday were any business of the Chancellor.

But when passing from these considerations, one reflects that although there was a free vote, measures such as the Abortion and Homosexuality Bills would not have got through under a Conservative House of Commons, that Court Lees would probably not have been closed by a Conservative Home Secretary, that the aerospace lobby is vociferously represented on the Conservative side and that the Party exhibits a strong desire to retain British troops as auxiliary policemen to the Americans all over the world, then any thought of association with it is impossible. It would be wrong to base one's politics on one's own professional speciality.

The greatest domestic political tragedy of the twentieth century is that the Conservatives rather than the Liberals emerged as the main anti-Socialist Party after the First World War. If the Liberals had stayed to occupy the place now held by the Conservatives they would, of course, have acquired many of the characteristics of the latter, and would by now be closely tied to capitalist and middle-class interest groups—in fact probably more so than the present-day Conservatives. But it is not too starry-eyed to suppose that they would exhibit less of the conformism, distaste for intellectual argument, and hierarchical outlook of the latter.

It will not have escaped the reader's attention that very little has been said about the modern Liberal Party with a capital 'L'.

The primary reason is that however much one may regret it, the political struggle does centre round the two main Parties. The Liberal Party is certainly not the cause of the malaise in British politics, but neither is it likely on the evidence of the post-war period to be an effective cure for it. There is another point that must in honesty be made. This is that the Party cannot be entirely identified with liberalism in the sense of personal freedom. The Liberals have paid a little too much regard to the left–right categorisation of the commentator. In the economic field this has at times made them excessively shy of proclaiming a belief in an intelligently managed free market lest it damage their claim to a left-wing label. They have also become too enraptured with syndicalist doctrines, such as co-ownership and workers' control. The trouble with such devices is that they tie the individual too closely to his place of work, and create an additional vested interest in preserving the industrial status quo. This aspect should not be overstressed. An entirely different flavour emerges from even the most anti-capitalist of the Young Liberals from that of socialist writers. Their concern for the individual shines through what they say and the last thing they want to do is to increase the power of the state or other communal organisations. Indeed their main anxiety is to give the worker more influence over his environment and less feeling of being a cog in an impersonal machine.

Differences about some of the policies advocated for achieving these aims should not deter anyone from joining the Liberal Party. The real reason for caution is, it must be faced, the two-party nature of the system. On any realistic view, it would be a mistake to become so committed to the Liberals that one lost all chance of influencing opinion in the two main parties. This consideration has been enormously reinforced by Mr Grimond's retirement, which carried the inescapable inference that he had given up hope of a realignment of parties around the Liberals.

The difficulty of political decisions in a two-party society cannot be easily cast aside even by the non-politicians. First there is the problem of voting. A rational egoist would not vote, but once a citizen has turned up at the booths, he ought logically to assume that the whole election hangs on his vote (leaving aside 'foregone conclusion' situations where the only uncertainty is the majority for the winning party). Those whose personal or professional interests are involved with questions of public policy face this difficulty in a specially acute form. A known but unobtrusive sympathy for one or other of the parties is undoubtedly a help. This not only provides more opportunities for conveying one's views to the political world, but it applies to social relations as well. There are for example many gatherings attended by those interested in economic policy, from private parties to formal meetings, where there is a predominantly right- or left-wing flavour in the room. The real embarrassment arises not for someone known to be on the other side, who will be treated with good-humoured tolerance, but for someone whose loyalty is felt to be uncertain or ambivalent.

There is a myth that political opponents are the greatest friends in private. Although personal enmities between politicians of different parties may not be as great as enmities within parties, this itself reflects the fact that they move in different circles. The Party division is also a social division (and here I mean 'social' not 'class'). It is easy to tell from the first glance at any gathering containing people in any way involved even on the fringes of politics whether it is predominantly a left-wing or a right-wing gathering.

There are of course many occasions—mainly Embassy functions, receptions for overseas visitors and parliamentary trips abroad, and to some extent the public rooms of the House of Commons—where members of both parties are thrown together. But with the exception of the last these are by their nature semi-official; and they are usually restricted fairly narrowly to MPs —or sometimes just to front-benchers. The vast mass of Fabians and Bow Groupers are confined to their own little worlds. Even at the top it is sheer romance to suppose that Labour and Conservative leaders are personal friends, or even well acquainted with each other off-duty in the way they often are among themselves. (The exception is the House of Lords, where Opposition Members may inform the Government spokesmen by telephone of the main points they intend to make and invite them down for weekends.) The result is that unless a determined effort is made to separate political from personal friendship, a choice of party is to some extent a choice of which company to keep; this must have had a decisive influence in a good many marginal cases.

There is in fact a good deal to be said for liberals with a small 'l' associating with one or other of the main parties. Yet unless they are sufficiently prominent in politics to be given office if an election goes the right way, there are always more important things to liberals than which of the two main parties is in power. It is certainly legitimate for egalitarian liberals to work through the Labour Party and anti-egalitarian liberals to work through the Conservatives. Indeed we should be in a poor way if liberals withdrew and left the collectivists and authoritarians in sole charge. Nevertheless for someone who is primarily a liberal, it can rarely be right to make too many concessions in his fundamental beliefs for the sake of the Party he has chosen as the lesser evil. A liberal who supports one of the two main parties should never regard the coming to power of the other party as the worst possible evil to reduce the chances of which every sacrifice is worth while. Loyalty is a virtue which is easily carried to excess at the expense of other and more important virtues.

A NOTE ON FREEDOM

A proper discussion of alternative definitions of freedom, and of suggestions for setting its limits, is outside the scope of this essay. A few words of explanation may however be in order. My own interpretation of freedom is that individuals should be allowed to run their own lives with the minimum of coercion. The basic notion is what Sir Isaiah Berlin has called 'negative freedom.' A man is said to be free to the degree to which no human being interferes with his activity.[13]

It is also associated with what Brian Barry has aptly labelled 'classical liberalism' in his book *Political Argument*.[14] This is the idea that 'the state is an instrument for satisfying the wants that men happen to have rather than of making good men.' The central belief can be most easily explained with the aid of two useful terms invented by Barry, 'want-regarding judgments' and 'ideal-regarding judgments.' Want-regarding principles take for granted the wants that people happen to have and concentrate on satisfying them. Ideal-regarding principles, on the other hand, do not accept that the individual's own preferences are sovereign; some wants are regarded as more worthy of gratification than others.[15] Classical liberalism pays attention only to want-regarding principles.

It is thus a variant of utilitarianism—providing the maximum of opportunities for people to have whatever it is that they want. (How these opportunities shall be distributed is a different question.) To justify giving this view the label 'liberalism' some restrictions are required. The wants in question must be confined to what Barry calls 'privately-oriented' ones. These are wants affecting oneself or one's family, which are contrasted with 'publicly oriented wants' which refer to a larger group. An example of the latter would be the intense 'want' felt by many respectable citizens for compulsory haircuts for the long-haired young. The exclusion of the latter type of want is justified on the grounds that so-called publicly oriented wants are really a disguised form of coercion. But in excluding them one is deliberately weakening the link between this 'liberal' variant of utilitarianism and any greatest happiness criterion—for it is all too easy to conceive of a community where the greatest happiness is derived by the majority from imposing their tastes on the minority.

Another restriction is that wants should be relatively 'self-determined.' A Brave New World, where the inhabitants are induced by hypnotic suggestions to want nothing but what they are going to be given, is not a liberal society. This restriction needs to be handled with care. There are those who extend the concept of hypnosis to the advertisements and mass media of present-day society, and use them as a pretext for saying that apparent consumer wants are not genuine and that other criteria should determine policy. The liberal, while aware of the danger, would regard the cure as worse than the disease and judge that the citizen, even in his present besotted state, should be left to make his own choices—perhaps with more advice from consumer associations, but with nothing more than advice.

Freedom should not be identified with the degree of want-satisfaction of any kind. For this would tie freedom too closely to prosperity, which is a different concept. But the extent to which policy is concerned with satisfying privately oriented wants rather than supposedly nobler objectives is one measure of its concern for freedom. This ties up with the non-coercion definition. For if the state tells people that certain wants are undesirable, whether by outright prohibition or discriminatory taxation, it is exerting a form of coercion. Freedom is not of course one-dimensional. A heavy tax on smoking is not on a par with Press censorship. But freedom to spend one's own money and time in one's own way is an aspect of freedom which is all too easily overlooked by one kind of radical.

Although the concept of freedom presented here is a little broader than Berlin's, it is still best described as 'negative' freedom. The absence of coercion is, however, an imprecise concept. The purest case of coercion would be where a person's hand is taken in a vice-like grip by some powerful human or automaton and physically forced to take action. But between this and the frown of an admired friend there is an infinite series of gradations. How about, for example, the power of an employer over an employee in a period of high unemployment and inadequate dole? The employee is free to depart and starve, just as a man can choose to be shot rather than do something at gun-point. But it is stretching words to say that coercion is absent in either case. Thus although it would be highly dangerous to accept a concept of 'positive' freedom, which would be identified with employment, prosperity or any other popular policy aim, the borderline between 'positive' and 'negative' freedom is far from easy to draw. I should myself be inclined to say that there is more freedom, even in the negative sense, in a fully employed than an under-employed economy, everything else being equal.

It is interesting that some on the Tory Right wing, who are far removed from economic liberalism, favour higher unemployment to preserve industrial discipline. Supporters of the market economy are split. Some of them are devotees of full employment. Others would like a larger margin of jobless, because they think this would reduce illiberal reliance on wage and price controls. Although I would myself disagree with this last school of thought, it is a perfectly legitimate assessment of the balance of risks.

Freedom cannot be absolute. It is a well-known paradox that some restraint on freedom is a condition for enjoying the freedom that remains. Despite all the criticisms that have been made of it, Mill's distinction between self-regarding and other-regarding actions is still one good test of where the line should be drawn. But it is not itself a sufficient safeguard. Even where it can be applied, the question of whether an action is self-regarding or other-regarding is one of degree. Moreover, a commitment to liberalism does not have to be all-or-nothing. Because I do not share Mr Hogg's punitive and repressive approach to drugs, I

do not feel compelled to advocate that heroin should be available
from slot-machines; and even though I prefer the risks of a consumer society to T. S. Eliot's more ordered vision, this does not
prevent me from supporting the few pence in tax we pay per
annum for the National Theatre, or Covent Garden, or the
National Gallery.* A liberal is someone who gives a relatively
high value to personal choice, not necessarily an absolute one.

Here again a concept from Brian Barry's extremely stimulating
and insufficiently discussed book can help. This is the idea of a
plurality of values which different people would choose to see
implemented in different proportions, as they cannot all be realised to the same degree simultaneously. The notion, which is
borrowed from the economist's indifference curves, measure a
person's preference for personal freedom, compared with, say
national military strength, when the two are in conflict, by asking
how much of the one he would accept as compensation for a
given loss of the other. This rate of exchange will not only vary
from person to person, but will vary according to the position on
the curve: the less freedom there is, the larger the gain in other
directions which will be needed to compensate for any further loss.
The bogey of how one measures freedom or military strength is no
obstacle to this technique which was devised by economists for
situations which could only be described in terms of more or less.

Finally, it is worth pointing out that a high weight can be
attached to freedom on a number of different grounds. In Brian
Barry's terminology freedom lies at the *confluence* of a number of

---

* There need be no inconsistency between a belief in free consumer choice
and advocacy of quite generous subsidies for the arts. I may want to support out
of my income performances of contemporary music, which I am too conservative in my tastes to patronise. There is nothing to prevent me subscribing
money; but my willingness to do so may be dependent on an assurance that
everybody else who wants to support a live musical culture will also contribute; and that the burden will not be concentrated among a few volunteers,
none of whom knows how much the others are subscribing. The theoretical
liberal answer would be a vast contract between the hundreds of thousands of
people concerned. But as this is not practical, some state support may give a
closer approximation to it than simple reliance on box-office receipts. The
more groups there are whose desires cannot be entirely expressed through
cash purchases, and the larger the proportion of the electorate they cover,
the more likely the above proposition is to be correct. (For example, another
person who has no wish to pay tax to support the arts may be quite happy to
do so to maintain public parks.)

ultimate considerations. Some people, myself included, would. regard negative freedom as a value in itself. It may be supported on the quasi-utilitarian grounds discussed above that 'want-satisfaction' (not happiness) will be maximised if desire to carry out actions which do not harm others is given free rein. This is even approximately true only if 'privately oriented' wants alone are allowed to count. Alternatively freedom can be supported because a high value is attached to variety and experimentation in ideas, works of art and styles of life. This variety may either be regarded as good in itself (an 'ideal-regarding' judgment), or as conducive to the community's long-term welfare. Different grounds can be given for supporting freedom in different situations.

8 / CONSENSUS: TRUE AND FALSE

How small, of all that human hearts endure
That part which laws or Kings can cause or cure.

SAMUEL JOHNSON, lines added to Goldsmith's *Traveller*

A QUESTION THAT WILL OCCUR to many readers is whether a simple piece of descriptive apparatus, such as the left–right spectrum, can be the cause of the British political malaise. The sceptic will rightly wonder whether it is at all likely that misuse of language is the main culprit. The real cause, it will be said, surely lies deeper. With this I would largely agree. The exaggerated and inappropriate use of the left–right dichotomy is in the main a symptom rather than a cause of whatever is wrong with British politics. But simple causality is rarely found in human affairs, whatever the case in the physical sciences. A perverse vocabulary of political comment can itself reinforce all the other forces corrupting the political dialogue and have a feedback effect. If the stereotyped labelling devices could be used less frequently, one would at least stop this reinforcement.

If this book has some slight influence in making people think twice before using left and right I will have every reason to feel satisfied. This is not as modest as it appears. For language and behaviour are so interrelated that it would be very difficult to have even a marginal effect on political terminology unless it were paralleled by some change, however minor, in political action. To use a Marxist metaphor, the language may be the superstructure, but changes in the superstructure react back on the base.

It is entirely appropriate to make armchair suggestions about the language and concepts of political discussion. These are matters on which there may be some hope of having a marginal influence. It would be quite another thing for someone outside the political arena, with no organised following, or means of influencing action, to set out ideas for a new political system. Even

Marx, who is always mentioned as an example of someone whose backroom writing changed the course of history, carefully avoided all temptations to provide a detailed picture of the Communist Utopia, and devoted most of his time to analysing the system he knew and its historical predecessors. This procedure is *a fortiori* sensible for lesser mortals with lesser ambitions.

I shall nevertheless mention in this chapter a few directions— some complementary, some alternative—in which British politics could evolve in a more hopeful direction. Many of the proposals are already part of the common coin of reformist literature. Any interest they may have to the reader will be in the selection made, and in the place they occupy in the general argument of this book. In putting forward ideas for change, it is essential to distinguish between forecasts of what will (or might) happen, and recommendations about what *ought* to happen, a distinction too frequently ignored even in the quality Press. This persistent trampling over Hume's distinction is not always due to ignorance of it. An old dictum in ethical theory is: 'Ought implies can.' This commands general acceptance, whether it is interpreted as deriving from the meaning of the word 'ought,' or as an ethical recommendation of its own. Transposing it to the future, one's recommendations should be taken from the family of things that might happen.

But what does 'might' mean? It would be profitless to limit the word simply to ruling out logical impossibilities. There is nothing self-contradictory about the idea that people might one day be able to fly without mechanical aids by waving their arms and legs, but for the purpose of making recommendations it can be safely treated as outside the range of possibilities. This is obviously a far-fetched example, but it is far from obvious where to draw the line. If one adopts a broad definition of 'things that might happen,' one might be tempted for example to advocate a Liberal Government (and of course tell the Liberals what liberalism is about), call for a much higher standard of party political debate, suggest new leaders for the existing parties, lay down a world disarmament plan, and table an indefinite number of other desirable suggestions. On the other hand, if one tries too hard to be realistic, one ends up simply trying to guess what the present leaders of the main parties might do, and selects one's recommendations from the two or three very slightly different courses of action from which one can at any time envisage these gentlemen actually choosing. The result can all too easily be that the writer aims at recommending what he thinks is going to happen anyway. Indeed the limitation of advice to 'what's on' is the besetting sin of British politics and journalism alike. The temptations in this direction are immense. The recommendation of a policy which is soon adopted gives the writer a flattering illusion of influence over events. Moreover the blurring of the distinction between recommendation and prediction is performed by the reader if the author does not oblige.

Many of the ills discussed in this book—the maximisation of spurious differences with the minimum of real conflict, the suppression of important issues and the separation by party or factional loyalties of people who ought to work together—owe their source to the excessive power of a certain type of party leader. This has been enormously enhanced by the highly personalised style of contemporary electioneering, which makes the Prime Minister the architect of electoral victory, and therefore the source of power, to a much greater extent than in the 1940s and 1950s, let alone the pre-war period. This exceptional power only evaporates when there has been a catastrophic falling away of popular support. If the rival party seems a reasonable bet for the next election, the Leader of the Opposition, who may be the source of future jobs and patronage, also has a very strong hold over his more ambitious supporters. It is true that the personalisation of politics is no ultra-modern phenomenon. Politics were dominated by the contest between party leaders in the age of Disraeli and Gladstone, and also perhaps in the Pitt–Fox era. The difference is that these historical figures were men of outstanding stature, whereas today the political battle would centre around *any* two men who happened to be Party Leaders. Once installed in No 10, the greatest mediocrity would wield enormous influence.

This does not mean that the Prime Minister will always get his way. He is far too busy being a 'whiz-kid' on a thousand different subjects to overcome really determined Civil Service resistance on any one of them. His main power is a negative one. Ideas can be cast aside, approaches blocked, individuals passed over, because the Party Leader does not care for them. Those with some knowledge of a particular subject may have the frustration of seeing their path blocked by the prejudices of two men, prejudices which may often coincide. This happened over economic policy in the period up to 1967, when both Mr Heath and Mr Wilson made the same error, imagining that there were things called 'fundamental structural reforms,' which could provide a quick way of escaping the choice between devaluation and relying on deflation alone.

One unfortunate effect of the present style of politics is that the kind of Leader is elected who thinks he must have a quick answer on every subject an interviewer chooses to raise, and who is temperamentally unable to delegate areas of policy where he has no competence or flair. This type of personality is normally vain, autocratic, intolerant of dissent and quick to interpret any criticism as a personal affront, or a plot against himself. The demand also appears to be for a person who prefers tangible details and administrative points to the logical analysis of policy alternatives, and who, perhaps for this reason, has a very possessive attitude towards his own lists of points, which he generally believes to differ profoundly from what the other side is or was doing.

It is interesting to speculate about what would have happened to British politics if two very different personalities, for example Mr Callaghan and Mr Maudling, had led the two parties. It is tempting to argue that, although the tendency towards an establishment consensus would have been even stronger than it is, at least the bitter pretence of a wide gulf between the two parties would have come to an end. With it might have gone the habit of denigrating everything that happens in Britain when the wrong party is in power. As a result of taking consensus to the limit, and making its existence obvious, the dissenters might have been forced into arguing outside the left–right framework, and political arguments would then have cut increasingly across traditional political alignments.

The trouble with this line of reasoning is that the choice of a Wilson–Heath rather than a Maudling–Callaghan type of leadership was not entirely an accident. If it were, it would be odd that the choice should have gone the same way in the two parties. The combination of industry, 'grittiness,' what passes for technocratic expertise, a strong autocratic instinct, and a 'Round-Britain Quiz' willingness to answer all questions on all subjects, seem to be at a premium in leadership contests. Above all—and this is what is so harmful to the more urbane approach—the party faithful demand a leader who will not permit either the similarities between the parties, or the impotence of conventional leadership in face of the combined influence of events and the Civil Service, to become too obvious.

This attitude reduced the chances of personalities cast in the Maudling or Callaghan mould. But even if one or both of them had become party leaders, there would have been enormous pressure on them to adopt a more partisan and 'grittier' style. One cannot assume that even Mr Gaitskell, if he had lived, would have been able to avoid these pressures altogether; and he himself was not entirely devoid of autocratic and intolerant instincts when his own conviction of the truth was at stake. It will be interesting to see how far Roy Jenkins will have to change his own cool and tolerant style in the direction of primitive point-scoring and partisanship, if supreme power moves closer to him.

One constitutional suggestion for reducing the excessive power of the Prime Minister has been advocated, among others, by Humphry Berkeley.[1] This would be to institute a fixed normal term of office for each Parliament. Such a change would, however, mainly reduce the power of the *Government* to secure its own re-election. Any reduction of the role of the Prime Minister would be at most indirect. Moreover, the Prime Minister and the Government would still be able to 'play politics' with the economy; there would merely be a reduction in their room for manœuvre, as they would have to work to a prescribed timetable. Fixed-term Parliaments are desirable not so much for any effect on the power of the Prime Minister but because they would provide an assured interval free from an electioneering atmosphere, which is lacking when there is uncertainty about the date of the poll.

The real problem is to ascertain what incentive a Government could ever have for introducing a change which would usually be against its interests. One possibility might be a situation in which the ruling party faced almost certain defeat, however late the election was called, and stood little to lose (*a*) from embarrassing its successor, and (*b*) from emphasising as a last throw its devotion to honest politics. Another possibility might arise if a party which had already had a good innings covering perhaps two full Parliaments already knew when it intended to call the next election, and wanted to increase its appeal by a fair-play gesture of this kind. There may be other eventualities. With any politically difficult suggestion, it is not possible to forecast the exact circumstances in which it might become practicable. The important thing is for the reformer to be ready to seize a favourable opportunity.

It would be wrong to pretend that fixed-term Parliaments would be more than a modest reform. The best hope for reducing the excessive influence of the two party leaders, without fundamental constitutional changes, lies in the vigilance of MPs. If sufficient Members of both parties are prepared to put their foot down against autocratic tendencies, excessive use of patronage, or the activities of a Prime-Ministerial *mafia*, they could have a very powerful effect. Not all Members are in a position to act in this way. MPs anxious for office or shadow office will tend to watch their step carefully. Although it is said that the path to the top is through rebellion, this is at best a half-truth. Mr Macmillan was kept in the wilderness for many years; rebelliousness was hardly the way to obtain promotion from Gaitskell, nor does it look like being the royal road to Mr Heath's favour. Although much has been made of Mr Wilson's skill in giving the 'Left' office, the people concerned usually had or acquired a personal loyalty to the Prime Minister, however unorthodox their views on party policy. These observations apply in normal times. Sinking ships suffer the same fate in politics as elsewhere.

The situation in the Labour Government in the abnormal circumstances of the early months of 1968, when Wilson's ascendancy disappeared, should turn out an interesting test case. The unanswered question was whether the undesirable aspects of one-man domination could be replaced by collective leadership without a complete loss of cohesion and disintegration of morale. The other question was whether, if Labour succeeded in weathering its difficulties, collective leadership could be sustained, or whether Mr Wilson, or some other leader, would not recover some of the old ascendancy.

Passing to a more technical level, one widely canvassed reform which might, if successful, help to redress the balance in favour of MPs and against both the Party Leaders and the Whitehall machine, would be the development of specialised Parliamentary committees. If these move in the right direction they could help bring out issues which the two front benches neglect, and may eventually even lead to cross-bench alliances. Open discussion of the assumptions and reasoning behind Civil Service advice would help particularly. For the present sterile party dialogue derives both from too ready an acceptance of at least the broad framework of this advice by Ministers, and from an excessive ignorance of, or contempt for, this advice by the same men when in Opposition. The more Whitehall discussion can be brought out into the open, the more will be known both of the real reasons for official policy and of the available alternatives.

It goes without saying that the issues involved are simultaneously political and technical; and there is not much hope for these committees unless they insist on qualified staff. There are many other snags *en route*. They will not achieve very much if they allow themselves to be prevented from probing too deeply on the grounds that they are getting into policy rather than administration. Nor will they be very successful, if they allow officials to take refuge behind the 'confidential nature of advice given to Ministers.' Then there are the siren voices telling them to stick to 'facts and figures,' or 'information.' But facts do not speak for themselves, and unless an attempt at analysis is made the reports will simply be praised for thoroughness and gather dust. A more insidious danger is that they will agree to treat on a confidential basis matters which Whitehall finds it convenient to suppress.

A different danger is that the committees might become pressure groups for specific interests. This risk could be minimised by setting up committees with broad functional responsibilities—such as foreign affairs, finance or the social services. In the USA the Senate Foreign Relations Committee is a more constructive body than service committees. It is no coincidence that it is on just these subjects that the party leaders are least anxious to see specialist committees operate. There may be a case for starting with closely circumscribed sectors such as agriculture or technology, for the sake of safety. But if the committees are not to disappoint all the hopes of the reformers they will have eventually to move on to larger and more contentious subjects.

Another danger is that the prospect of office may blunt the zeal of Government—and perhaps even of Opposition—backbenchers. There is no quick answer to this. The only sure safeguard is to build up the prestige of these committees until the chairmanship of one of them is either in itself a recommendation for a Cabinet job, or offers a worth-while position in itself, fully competitive in attractions with all but the top few Government posts. It would help to increase the attractions if there were normally a vice-chairman from the Opposition. The problem then would be how to escape the American danger of too many committees dominated by very senior and elderly reactionaries. One possibility might be to limit the tenure of the chairmanship and vice-chairmanship to a maximum of a few years. Another problem is the appointment of chairmen. Both seniority and relying on the party whips could be dangerous; and there might be something to be said for genuine election by the members.

The real test of whether the committees can contribute anything to *political* life will show in the way they vote. If they divide on strictly party lines we will know the worst. But equally, if their reports are unanimous, we will know that they are playing safe. The day that signatures from both parties are found together on either a majority or minority report on a major issue, a political breakthrough will have been made. Until then the contribution of the committees will be ancillary.

Political reform cannot, however, be left solely to specialised Parliamentary committees, both because of the risk that they will not live up to expectations, and because effective change will still have to come from the main political arena. Once the novelty is over, it is easy to imagine committee reports attracting less and less attention, and Ministers becoming increasingly indifferent to their findings. More directly political changes are also required.

Such changes ought to have as their aim a breakdown of the present absurd rigidity of the two-party system. Ronald Butt has referred to the 'paradox of the British post-war pattern of politics,' in which 'the Conservative and Labour Parties have been moving closer together in terms of practical policies,' but total commitment to a single party, 'however loudly a Member may disagree with aspects of its thinking, is accounted on all sides a supreme political virtue.'[2] Mr Butt points out that the handful of Members who have crossed the floor of the House since the Second World War have sunk without a trace.[3] A further stultifying influence is that the composition of the two main Parliamentary parties is, as Mr Butt has put it, largely 'determined at the roots of the party in the country—and it is, after all, from such parliamentary parties so constituted that Prime Ministers and Ministers are eventually selected.' In fact the main obstacle to candidates outside the normal party stereotypes is usually to be found at the local level.[4]

There are two approaches towards loosening the rigidity of the two-party system. One would be to make it easier for third or fourth parties, or for men with blurred or non-existent party allegiances, to play a part in politics. The other would be to accept the two-party system, but to attempt to modify its nature. The most important single step in the former direction, away from a strict two-party system, would be the introduction of either the Alternative Vote or the Single Transferable Vote. The great advantage of both systems is that they would eliminate the fear of the wasted vote. Under the Alternative Vote, which is extremely simple to operate, supporters of minority candidates would know that if their first choice came bottom of the poll, their second choice would count . . . and so on until only two contestants remained. The Single Transferable Vote (STV) is more complicated to operate and would require multi-member constituencies. But it has many additional advantages. It would prevent the waste of votes not merely for the candidates at the bottom of the list, but would redistribute the surplus votes of the candidates at the top as well. Unlike the Alternative Vote, the STV would enable minorities to secure representation and would enable voters to express preferences between the candidates of their own party.[5]

If there were no change in voting habits as a result, the Liberals would be the obvious beneficiaries of either system. It is usually argued, I think correctly, that the change in the system would encourage more people to vote for Liberal candidates, other smaller parties and independents, because they would no longer be afraid to waste their votes; and that the calculations which are sometimes made of Parliamentary representation, under AV or STV, understate the likely changes.

On the other hand an ingenious argument can be constructed to show that the smaller parties would actually lose if the electoral law were changed. There are at present a number of constituencies where only one of the two major parties stands any chance of winning. It may not in fact succeed, but the other party is not a runner at all. Examples include Welsh constituencies where a Conservative vote is a wasted vote, or suburban areas such as Orpington where the same might be said of a Labour vote. However much an anti-Conservative in Orpington might see a general election as a plebiscite between two alternative Governments, it would be pretty pointless to vote Labour and his most rational course would be to vote for the present Liberal Member, Eric Lubbock. Similar considerations might lead a strong anti-Socialist to vote Welsh Nationalist in some constituencies. Under a reformed and fairer system in which no vote were wasted, things would be different and those who think in plebiscitary terms would have every incentive to confine their choice to the two main parties.[6]

My own guess, however, is that starting from a position where, after the last election, only 13 out of 630 seats were held by Liberals and others, a change in the system would help the smaller parties. I doubt if electors are so 'rational' that they will throw away the chance of voting Liberal, Nationalist, or for any other minority, once their vote is no longer 'wasted' in an obvious sense. Moreover, once the smaller battalions had achieved a breakthrough, and a House were elected with no single party in absolute command, minority voters would rapidly gain in confidence and would be much less inclined to think in plebiscitary terms. How near such breakthrough might be is shown by a calculation suggesting that, on the assumption of no change in votes cast, Labour would only have had under STV a bare majority over all others combined even at the time of its great victory in 1966.[7] (Under AV, there would have been a few more Liberals, but the gains would nearly all have come from the Tories.)

I would suspect that once the system had been run in, not merely the Liberals, but all unorthodox candidates would benefit. A Conservative MP disowned by his local association could appeal directly to the electorate without fear of splitting his Party's vote. A Labour supporter who disapproved of Government support for US Vietnam policies could stand on an independent ticket without fear of letting the Tories in. In a similar way anti-Common Market candidates would have a chance. These effects would apply much more strongly under STV than AV, but even the smaller change would have a noticeable effect.

The very reason why electoral reform is popular with the Liberals makes it unpopular with the two main parties. Yet one can imagine situations in which reforms would interest the majority party of the day. A Prime Minister who saw a bid for Liberal and independent goodwill as his best way of preventing otherwise near-certain defeat at the next election, might consider the idea seriously. The Wilson Government put out a feeler in that direction at quite an early stage in its career. Moreover electoral change, introduced unilaterally by a Labour Government, involving no obligation to anyone, ought surely to be less repugnant to Labour MPs than the formal Liberal Alliance proposed by Woodrow Wyatt in 1964-6. But if anything is to happen, thinking and planning will have to start immediately among supporters of the idea in both Labour and Liberal parties.

All this assumes that electoral reform is desirable, a point which would be disputed by many political experts. They fear that if electoral reform were to achieve its objectives absolute majorities would be the exception rather than the rule and the normal state of affairs would be a coalition or a minority Government. A coalition could mean either a combination of some parties or elements (say the much-discussed radical alliance) or something much more widely embracing, containing both Labour and Conservative members. Thus a verdict cannot be given on electoral reform without discussing the case for one or other type of coalition, in any case a perennially topical subject.

It should be said at the outset that the kind of businessman's coalition discussed in some circles at the beginning of 1968, involving newspaper proprietors and chairmen of nationalised industries, would be worse than the disease it is designed to cure. Apart from its anti-democratic and even dictatorial overtones— if the idea were taken seriously—there was not the slightest reason to suppose that the group of people in question would have done any better than conventional politicians. The problems of government are inherently different from those of running a business; and any 'Great Britain Ltd' type of Government would become even more dependent on Civil Service briefs, which it would carry out more woodenly, than any ordinary Government. The fact that the idea could have had such an airing, however, reflects a very reasonable public distaste for the recent conduct of both parties.

The arguments for and against a predominantly political coalition are more finely balanced. Such a Government would curtail one of the evils of the present style of Party politics mentioned in earlier chapters: the denigration of everything that goes on in the country by one party when the other is in power. Indeed a major objection often raised is that 'consensus' attitudes would become virtually unchallengeable. While the coalition lasted, there would be no effective vehicle for attacking Government policies of the day and the electorate might be even more tempted to turn in disillusionment against all politicians. But I rather doubt whether the voices of dissent would be any less effective than they are today. In some ways a coalition would make obvious the real nature of the issues at present obscured by the sham party war. If the leading orthodox politicians of both parties were in the Government, there would be less excuse for supposing that the disliked policies were due to the fact that the wrong party was in power, and there would be less temptation for critics to subordinate their more individual views to the general lines of their party's policy.

A much more difficult argument to meet is that coalition governments would not in practice be strong governments, as they would be concerned to avoid at all costs anything that might break up the coalition; and would therefore make even more concessions to interest groups, and concentrate even more on public relations, than single-party administrations. One might ask what the position of a Labour Government would be if not even the nominal allegiance of Labour Members could be relied upon, and there had to be a series of formal bargains with each faction before a policy could be adopted or a Bill tabled.

Neither historical evidence nor the experience of other countries provides a conclusive test. One has to go back to the 'confusion of parties' between 1846 and 1868 to find an extended period of coalitions or minority Governments in Britain. (The National Government of the 1930s, the Lloyd George–Conservative Administration after the First World War and the Conservative–Liberal-Unionist alliance at the turn of the century were basically all Conservative Governments.) The apparent disintegration of the two-party system in the mid nineteenth century was intensely disliked by politicians such as Salisbury and Disraeli and severely criticised by the political journals.[8] But it is doubtful if this was more than a professional inconvenience. There is no evidence that England was less well governed or that the debate on policy was more stifled than in the earlier or later parts of the century. Although there were many things that needed putting right there were no great issues of a popular kind around which the two parties could have divided. There was no harm in the mid-Victorian consensus expressing itself in a political coalition; at least outsiders, whether Marx, Mill or Ruskin, saw exactly where they stood and based no false expectation on General Election results.

Contemporary Western European experience can be interpreted almost according to taste. In some countries, notably in Scandinavia, a multi-party system and coalition governments have been accompanied by political stability; in others further south they have not. It is, however, worth glancing at the recent experience of Germany and France. The German Grand Coalition between Christian and Social Democrats, formed at the end of 1966, has been subject to much internal strain and may not be in existence by the time these words are published. It has been criticised for leaving the dissenters with nowhere to go, and also on the wider ground that it is too soon after 1945 for Germany to abandon the Government and Opposition dialogue.

It is less usual to mention the achievements of the Grand Coalition. The first steps were taken away from a narrow obsession with budget-balancing towards a Keynesian full-employment policy. The shift in political allegiance towards France is too commonly criticised through British eyes. The Grand Coalition in fact brought to an end a long period of unhealthily large dependence on the United States; and the Kiesinger policy did give the Federal Republic, for the first time since the War, a genuinely European orientation. Nor was the political atmosphere in Germany more authoritarian than during the long period of the Adenauer ascendancy. Another interesting feature was the notable difference in policies between the coalition and its Erhard–Schröder predecessor. This suggests that differences inside the Christian Democrats—which are not easily classifiable on a right–left axis—are in some way greater than those between Christian and Social Democrats.

General de Gaulle's Government in France has also many of the features of a coalition in the sense, not of an all-party government, but of one embracing a number of different elements. The Gaullists range right across the spectrum in conventional right–left terms, and would have been scattered throughout all the other parties if their movement had not existed. If they survive the General, it will be as a force emphasising unity, cohesion and strong government as against the party political game.

In the heyday of the de Gaulle regime, policy was determined by the interplay between a strong president and a strong bureaucracy, with a popular check provided by plebiscites and presidential elections. The general label Caesarianism would probably apply, except that the element of vulgarity was lacking. This is not a system which it would be desirable to copy in Britain. But the French did manage to withdraw from overseas commitments, reform the economy, and establish an independent position from the United States many years before a British Government brought itself to do some of the same things. The General was helped in these directions by his freedom from the prejudices and pressure groups which slowed down similar British action but had no real basis in the genuine interests of any section of the British population. The question is whether we can learn anything from his successes without emulating the less desirable features of his regime.

Many professional politicians will, however, wonder how any sort of coalition, whether partial or all-embracing, could ever be inaugurated in Britain as it is so much against the personal interests of the leaders of both parties. There is too great a temptation to take Ramsay MacDonald and the events of 1931 as a prototype. History, however, may not repeat itself quite so neatly. My own suspicion is that if a coalition comes at all it will (leaving aside electoral reform) be as a result of a Tory split. This may seem to contradict my earlier strictures on the excessive conformism among Conservatives; but things change, and there are tensions below the surface which could get out of control when the party is next in office.

On balance, I would regard an experimental interval of coalition government as desirable in Britain if—and only if—one constitutional convention is altered. This is the one under which the life of a Government is threatened when it is defeated on a major issue. If this convention remained, many of the advantages claimed for a coalition of any kind would vanish, and it might well turn out to be weak, rather than strong, government, and even more 'political' in the bad sense of the word than a party Government. The same qualification applies also to any recommendation for electoral reform. A new convention would be required under which it would need a general vote of censure to unseat a Government. Such a change in the rules would be far more than a technicality; it would have the most profound impact on the whole political game. It would throw open a whole range of issues, now decided by the Government, to a House of Commons vote. Instead of the Cabinet and Civil Service making nearly all policy, subject only to the need not to strain the loyalty of the ruling party to breaking point, many key decisions would depend on the changing combination of Parliamentary factions and individuals. If such a system were grafted on to our existing institutions, the result would indeed be weak, vacillating and inconsistent government. To prevent this even more far-reaching changes would be required. Peter Pulzer has pointed out that in most Continental countries with multi-party systems, there is a sharp distinction between party and state, between the politicians on the one hand and the bureaucratic machine on the other.[9] It can be argued that this distinction, whatever its origins, reflects the complex technical realities of twentieth-century government rather better than the British one. If the Cabinet of the day is no longer to have an almost automatic majority in the House, this will have to be accompanied by a much more explicit recognition of the role of the Civil Service in formulating policy, especially in its long-term aspects; and a willingness on the part of the legislature to allow the bureaucracy some formal as well as practical initiative. Such a recognition of reality, far from weakening democratic control, might actually enhance it. The great myth that Civil Servants are servile eunuchs of all-powerful Ministers enables the former to exercise power without effective challenge or scrutiny. It might be healthier for all concerned if the role of officials as 'permanent politicians'[10] were to be made explicit and subject to more Parliamentary scrutiny.

Before this could happen, yet another fundamental change of attitude would be required among politicians and among informed opinion. It would be necessary to drop the pretence that the whole of Britain's economic and social structure is liable to be overturned if the complexion of the Government changes. There is in fact already a consensus, embracing the bulk of potential Ministers in all parties, on many matters of economic and social policy, even though the nature of this consensus changes slowly with time. Paradoxically, the refusal to recognise it smothers debate on the real disagreements which ought to be aired at a political level. I shall return to the need for a 'public philosophy' in my concluding paragraphs. For it so happens that similar, if less drastic, changes would be required if the alternative approach to reform—accepting the two-party system, but attempting to loosen it up—is to succeed. I now therefore turn to this second avenue.

One of the most frequently canvassed institutional reforms for reducing some of the extreme rigidity of the two-party system is the institution of primary elections by local parties as a method of picking their candidates, as in the United States. At present the few thousand local activists who select the candidates have much greater influence on the composition of the House of Commons than the mass electorate who choose between the party labels. These activists, whom Peter Paterson has christened the 'selectorate,'[11] tend by their very nature to be enthusiastic supporters of traditional Party attitudes—egalitarian and anti-profit in the Labour Party and hawk-like defenders of private property among Conservatives.*

The question about primaries is whether throwing the choice open to a few thousand *party members* in each constituency would lead to a better or more representative choice of candidate than leaving the selection to a few *activists*. There is the possibility that the small minority of intense activists will, because they are more politically knowledgeable, be more inclined on occasion to give a chance to the untypical candidate, who would not show up well in a popularity poll among the less active party members. Related to this is the danger that the primary might encourage the organisation man who takes his party platform for granted (although resolutely 'empirical' in office), and devotes all his energies to a whole hierarchy of campaigns, first for selection, then for election and eventually for Ministerial office.

The balance of advantage is likely to vary enormously from constituency to constituency. The 'primary' among Tories in Bournemouth East some years ago showed that the liberal-minded Nigel Nicolson had much more support among party members than among the inner caucus, even though the vote went against him. The results are likely to depend in part on the number of new members who would be attracted into the political parties from outside the range of orthodox party-liners. (For one must

---

* Professor Richard Rose has shown that the majority of resolutions submitted to annual conferences by local parties are not of an extremist kind.[12] They either voice agreed party policy, or uncontroversial generalities. This does not in my view invalidate the common-sense observation that traditional party attitudes are genuinely and wholeheartedly endorsed, in pretty well unreconstructed form, by constituency activists—more so than among any other section of the population.

assume that—to begin with at any rate—British primaries would be 'closed.') Mr Paterson rightly regards the possible increase in party membership as one of the main planks in his case for primaries. For paradoxically, those who are most sceptical of the traditional Labour–Conservative dogfight should be keennest to join one or other political party to end their present disenfranchisement. If primaries become at all widespread, it would be thoroughly logical—and not in the least insincere—for the independent, liberal voter to join the predominant party in a safe constituency, and thereby exercise some influence on the composition of the House of Commons.

The tendency could go even further. Committed Socialists might be tempted to register as Conservatives in constituencies such as South Kensington, and vice versa in the safe Labour seats. I doubt, however, whether this would do much harm. If such infiltrators use their influence in the right spirit, the result could be an increase in the variety and types of attitudes represented in Parliament. If infiltrators from the other party go too far and actually attempt to use their influence to secure a bad or unattractive candidate, there should be no difficulty in defeating them by sheer weight of numbers.

The advantage of primaries is that they can be introduced experimentally in some constituency parties, and one might hope to end up with a blend of different methods of selection. The case for them is strongest in safe constituencies, partly because perverse tactical infiltration can be most easily defeated in them. In addition, the voter without very strong party loyalties will be less hesitant about committing himself to a single party when he knows that the other party does not stand the slightest chance at the real Parliamentary election. On balance I would like to see the idea tried on an experimental basis. The beauty of the primary idea is that, alone of the widely canvassed reforms, it does not have to be initiated by the leadership of either main party and can be introduced by sufficiently determined local initiative. The obstacle is that party stalwarts would have to give up voluntarily the one real political power they have, that of selecting candidates. Nevertheless, it might be a tempting way out for associations with severe internal divisions. There would also be some kudos to be gained for the pioneers; there would be plenty of controversial questions concerning the running of the primaries to bolster the ego of the stalwarts; and once a few primaries had been held, fashion could make the habit spread.

The reader may nevertheless share my suspicion that neither primary elections nor any other purely mechanical devices, however valuable, will do enough to break down the conventional left–right pattern of political dialogue, and that more fundamental change will also be required even if the two-party system is retained. One approach would be to look for ways of encouraging political discussion outside the framework of the parties. An example would be the US debate on Vietnam, which has ranged right across party, and in which Democrats and Republicans have not been afraid to join together in opposition to colleagues from their own parties.

One possibility in the United Kingdom might be the development of non-party bodies, such as the Anti-Corn-Law League of the 1830s and 1840s, to campaign on specific political issues. The nearest equivalent in recent times has been the Common Market Campaign, in which politicians of all parties, together with businessmen, academics and others, were highly successful in mobilising 'opinion formers' (although not in securing British entry). There have been other less clear-cut non-party lobbies in recent years. The setting up of the National Economic Development Council in 1962, and the conversion of the last Conservative Government to indicative planning, was the result of a fairly apolitical revulsion against stop-go and the desire for a more expansionist approach. The main conversion that took place was not that of any political party, but of the Federation of British Industries. Like the Common Market campaign, it was more successful in influencing opinion-formers than in affecting the actual course of events.

But the mention of these two non-party pressure groups is, however, sufficient to bring out their limitations in present conditions. The economic growth lobby of the early 1960s was only held together by a failure on the part of many of the industrialists and politicians who supported it to think through their slogans to a logical conclusion. In particular they had not faced up to the probable need—which should have been apparent from the very beginning—to choose between economic expansion and the maintenance of the old sterling parity. Moreover as the 1964 election approached some supposedly expansionist economists became more interested in discrediting the Conservative Government than in promoting their own declared economic beliefs. On the other side of the fence many Conservatives, in both the House of Commons and the City, were all too easily brainwashed by Mr Wilson into believing that the whole growth experiment had been shamefully irresponsible.

A possible moral is that cross-bench movements are under a grave handicap in periods such as the present where a change of Government is never far from the horizon, but may have a better chance during a period of apparent one-party rule such as the aftermath of the 1959 election. This links up with what was said in an earlier chapter about the greater susceptibility of Civil Servants and Ministers in those years to pressures other than those of the opinion polls or television ratings. Greater enterprise in forming cross-bench movements and alliances might even now yield worth-while results. But it would be idle to expect an early return to political quietism. Such periods are not in any case likely under Labour Governments, however ineffective the official Opposition; and even if the Conservatives are returned at the next election the activist style of opposition inaugurated by Mr Wilson is unlikely to be cast aside quickly.

Ultimately a move towards a more relevant form of political discussion in a two-party system must depend on an evolution in the nature of the parties themselves. In particular, it requires a more realistic recognition by the parties of changes which are already taking place in the nature of their struggle. Perhaps in an ideal system it would be better if the party conflict corresponded with the real argument over policy—assuming that there were one overriding argument to which the others could be related. But as a very good second best, there is something to be said for the other extreme in which people going into politics do not have to put up a pretence of sharing a series of profound convictions with other members of their party, but could instead frankly recognise it as a game of 'ins' and 'outs.' Allegiance could then be determined— as it is already, but with greater frankness—on considerations such as which social *ambiance* the aspiring politician preferred, or on which seemed to be the winning side.

One way by which the smokescreen of ideology might be removed would be a more open recognition of the interest group basis of the two main parties. The Labour Party would only attempt to be distinctive on issues affecting trade unions, or the distribution of incomes between the manual working class and the rest of the population. The Conservatives would remember their middle-class clients; but beyond this there would be no attempt at distinctive Conservative foreign policy or Labour economic policy; the party leaders would make a selection from the ideas that happen to be in the air, by the normal mixture of genuine conversion and electoral expediency. This is of course to a large extent what already happens. But if the pretence of something different were dropped, so far from this being a victory for pragmatism (so-called) the way would be open for genuine arguments over ideas and principles on a cross-bench basis.

In one sense, the present party battle is moving even further away from the traditional model than the preceding paragraph suggests, as the two main parties seem prepared to risk the loyalty of their own interest groups for the sake of a broader appeal. With the domination of television and the personalisation of politics around the leaders, the temptation grows to concentrate on nation-wide appeals divorced from the class basis of the parties. The party leaders would really like to have it both ways: in the case of the Labour Party to make a broad popular, even anti-union appeal, in 'presidential' broadcasts, while cementing the loyalty of the traditional trade union and working-class supporters at occasions like party conferences. For the latter purpose, it seems necessary to keep up the pretence of two totally different ideologies. The shock to the army of devoted party workers on both sides, if it were openly admitted that they were simply the forces of Tweedledum and Tweedledee, would be shattering; and they sometimes seem prepared to go to any length of self-delusion to protect themselves from this knowledge. An example was the pathetic shock of Labour Party delegates at the Scarborough Conference of 1967 when the Governor of the Bank of England spelled out that the Government's then policy of 're-deployment' really meant running the economy with a higher margin of unemployment than in the past.

Owing to these powerful emotional vested interests, it will be a long and gradual process before a more realistic view of the party battle can come to be admitted. A major policy move by a Labour Prime Minister who went too far in alienating his traditional supporters but nevertheless survived, or an imaginative gesture by a Conservative leader towards radicals in all parties, would speed up the process. So would a nation-wide cross-bench controversy which stirred people's imagination more than the Common Market did, and was less impossibly technical than devaluation. (One hopes that the race issue will not assume this role.)

Part of the trouble with the existing situation is that it is a halfway house. We have gone a long way towards replacing a conflict of ideologies by a system of 'ins' and 'outs.' If we went the whole hog, then arguments over policy could at last be separated from the party conflict, and we would be nearer a Democrat-versus-Republican situation. The separation would not be total. Partisans of particular policies would fight to capture the party leaderships; but there would be no longer the automatic assumption voiced by Mr Cousins at Scarborough that the only alternative to Mr Wilson was Mr Heath who would be worse. At the time of writing it is an open question whether the US Republican presidential candidate will be more 'dove-like' or 'hawk-like' than Johnson. The odds of course are that, if the Vietnam War continues, he will try to have it both ways and give the impression that he stands a better chance both of negotiating a peace and of winning the Vietnam War than his Democratic opponent. In 1960 John Kennedy both rallied the hawks with an alarm about a non-existent missile gap, while at the same time indicating that he would be more adventurous in seeking agreement with the Russians. Similarly in 1952 Eisenhower promised to end the Korean War without indicating whether this would be by negotiation or escalation.

In the early part of 1968 the 'doves' (not that they were organised in one body) were free to try either to gain the Republican nomination or capture the Democratic nomination from Johnson, or both. All this is no doubt very confusing to those who like neat patterns, especially as the two presidential platforms are likely to turn out almost identical (the 1964 Goldwater campaign was a sport). The flexibility of the US party system undoubtedly leaves the way open for a much freer discussion of issues than in Britain.

The main obstacle to a loosening of party rigidity in this country is the myth that the two parties stand for utterly different ways of regulating the country's internal affairs. As long as this myth is upheld, Labour and Conservative will be seen as doctrinal parties; and so long as they are regarded in this way the emphasis will be put on the narrow range of issues and slogans on which each party can unite against its opponents. Thus we arrive at the paradoxical conclusion that, to undermine the false consensus which inhibits political discussion of many key issues, the genuine consensus which exists on many subjects normally at the heart of party political debate needs to be brought out into the open. Or to look at the matter in another way: if the two parties gave up the pretence of being united by a common set of beliefs and values, if people and groups co-operated within and across parties in unpredictable and changing combinations, as I am advocating, there would be a real danger of loss of all sense of coherence and direction, unless behind all the debate there were some common public philosophy.

The consequences of the sudden disappearance of all traditional party guidelines, in favour of *ad hoc* empiricism, became all too clear in the collapse of Labour Party morale at the beginning of 1968. I happen to think that the new post-devaluation policies are superior both to traditional Labour beliefs and to the ill-conceived 'physical planning' of 1964–7. Properly explained, they ought moreover to harmonise with the underlying value-judgments of most Labour MPs, even if not with the policies which they had hitherto embraced to give effect to these judgments. It is an advantage, not a disadvantage, that such policies ought also to be acceptable to many Conservative supporters of a market economy, if only they were prepared to go back to first principles (I make an exception in this praise for the over-zealous pursuit of an 'incomes policy.' This has been called a 'dangerous nonsense,' but I would put the emphasis on the second word.

These latest policies would not have come as such a shock to Labour MPs if the attempt at rethinking the party's philosophy, begun in the Gaitskell era, had not been so quickly abandoned. In the short term it is always easier for professional politicians to regard the deep-seated beliefs of their own party as so much 'theology,' on which the less said the better. But on a longer view, it might actually pay party leaders to attempt to argue with, persuade and educate people whose beliefs they regard as mistaken, rather than to attempt to bedazzle with a display of instant activity. An additional trouble in 1968 was that the new policies were forced on the Government as the result of the failure of its original approach, and not because of the conscious adoption of a more up-to-date outlook—a further symptom of the same malaise.

A great deal of harm was in fact done by Labour's contemptuous dismissal in the run-up to the 1964 election of everything that had previously been done in economic management, in industrial and scientific policy and in the social services, in the sincere but erroneous belief that it had better and more professional alternatives. The Conservatives have unfortunately taken a leaf out of Mr Wilson's 1964 book and are offering an equally improbable computerised revolution in the running of our affairs should they win the next election. These tedious diversions obscure the fact that the management of demand, Government relations with industry, the encouragement of investment, regional development, science policy and many similar activities are hardly at issue between the parties. A great deal of the burden in these spheres inevitably falls on officials; and intellectual fashion plays a much greater part in them than the results of elections. The pretence that these are highly partisan issues and that the Opposition of the day has brilliant new techniques for coping with them prevents genuine issues of principle from being discussed. During the first three years of the Labour Government the whole question of Britain's role in the world, sterling and the sterling area, and the political choices involved in opting for Europe—all subjects on which no actual consensus existed—were swept under the table in the interests of a pseudo-debate on what were really consensus subjects. Even in internal policy, fundamental issues such as the distribution of income and wealth, the purpose and future of the social services, and personal choice versus paternalism, were put aside in favour of empty and banal arguments about 'cuts' and 'economies,' which could not be sensibly discussed except in relation to these wider issues.

The end of one book is not the place to begin on another and there is no space to describe in any detail the economic and social philosophy that could be accepted by a majority of informed opinion in both parties. But the basic elements are not difficult to find. The germ of a new public philosophy on social and economic policy is I believe already contained in Professor John Rawls's idea of the four branches of government.[13] (These branches are purely conceptual, not suggestions for actual organisation.) The first is the *allocation* branch, designed to keep the economy reasonably competitive. It is also charged with correcting, where possible by taxes and subsidies, the more glaring gaps between private and social costs and benefits. Secondly, the *stabilisation* branch aims to maintain some compromise between full employment and price stability. Thirdly, the *transfer* branch guarantees a minimum level of material well-being, either by paying out benefits, or by a negative income tax. The fourth *distribution* branch operates a system of inheritance and gifts taxes designed to prevent undue concentration of economic power. If it is sufficiently successful here, its other job of raising state revenue could best be carried out by proportional taxes on expenditure in place of progressive income tax or surtax.

Clearly there is room for a great deal of argument about detail, application and questions of degree. These are profitable subjects for Parliamentary discussion, although not always in plenary session. But suitably expounded and elaborated, I believe that some 75–80 per cent of the political world could be persuaded to accept some 75–80 per cent of this approach. Like all attempts at logical clarification, it should lead not merely to a compendium of existing policies, but to an improvement on them. Even the desperately brief summary just given suggests a fruitful way out of the barren controversy about the sharing of the national cake. For it suggests that instead of having to choose between incentive and 'social justice' there could be more of both simultaneously.

The acceptance of a public philosophy of this kind would leave more, rather than less, to argue about. The nature and amount of redistribution of wealth, the balance between paternalism and leaving people to spend their own money, the location of the compromise between price stability and full employment, the allocation of public funds between different amenities, would all stand out more clearly as subjects for political discussion once the unnecessary undergrowth had been cleared. Controversies would also sometimes arise from major illogicalities within the machine, such as the absence of any regulator for keeping this country in economic balance with the rest of the world. But the main advantage of accepting a more articulated and coherent version of the mixed economy is that energies would be freed to other and more fruitful subjects ranging from Britain's position in the world, to more general argument about the type of society we want.

The argument has come full circle. This book began as a protest against the whole constricting concept of the 'battle for the centre' which arises from the left–right view of politics. Yet the argument has shown that if there is to be more scope for public discussion outside the narrow range separating the two party leaders, if seemingly extreme ideas are to be seriously debated before they become fashionable, and if desirable policy changes are to be carried out in time instead of several years too late, it is all the more important to have a corpus of widely accepted belief. This is not a matter of forcing ideas on people against their convictions, but of accepting agreement where agreement exists, or is obscured merely by a difference of language. A healthy society does not pretend that a revolution in its economic and social institutions is likely every four or five years. The real antidote to false consensus is the courage not to manufacture disagreements where none exist.

REFERENCES

INTRODUCTION

1. David Butler: 'The Paradox of Party Differences,' p. 266, *Studies in British Politics* (edited by Richard Rose); Macmillan, 1966.

2. Charles Taylor: 'Neutrality in Political Science,' Chapter 2 of *Philosophy, Politics and Society*, Third Series (edited by P. Laslett and W. G. Runciman); Basil Blackwell, 1967.

3. See for instance *Economic Forecasts in Member Countries*, published by OECD, Paris 1965. (Available from HMSO.)

1 / THE LEFT–RIGHT CONFUSION

1. Ian Trethowan: 'MPs at Battle Stations,' *The Times*, 23 February 1967.

2. Ronald Butt: 'Whatever happened to that "great debate"?' *Financial Times*, 3 March 1967.

3. Milton Friedman: *Sunday Telegraph*, 25 June 1967.

4. D. E. Butler and A. King: *The British General Election of 1964*, p. 54; Macmillan, 1965.

5. Rudolf Klein: 'Red Guards for Thorpe,' *Observer*, 2 January 1967.

6. Victor Zorza: *Guardian*, 5 July 1967.

2 / WORDS AND IDEAS

1. *Dictionary of the Social Sciences*, p. 381 *et seq.*; Tavistock Publications, 1964. (Entry by William Pickles: 'Left and Right.')

2. Philip Converse: 'The Nature of Belief Systems in Mass Publics,' in *Ideology and its Discontents* (edited by David Apter); Free Press, 1964.

3. James Littlejohn: 'The Choreography of "Left Hand and Right",' *New Society*, 9 February 1967.

4. *The European Right* (edited by Hans Rogger and Eugen Weber); Weidenfeld & Nicolson, 1965.

5. Kingsley Amis: 'Why Lucky Jim Turned Right,' *Sunday Telegraph*, 2 July 1967.

6. J. L. Talmon: *The Origins of Totalitarian Democracy*; Secker & Warburg, 1952.

7. David Caute: *The Left in Europe*, p. 38; World University Library, 1966. (My indebtedness to this useful volume will be apparent through the chapter.)

8. Converse: in *Ideology and its Discontents*.

9. S. Beer: *Modern British Politics*; Faber 1965.

10. Caute: *The Left in Europe*.

11. Maurice Duverger: *The Idea of Politics*, p. 141; Methuen, 1966.

12. Roy Jenkins, in an interview with Kenneth Harris, *Observer*, 10 December 1967.

13. D. E. Butler and Anthony King: *The British General Election of 1966*, p. 124; Macmillan 1966.

14. Blondel: *Voters, Leaders and Parties*, pp. 42–8; Penguin, 1966.

15. Beer: *Modern British Politics*.

3 / THE CONCEPTS IN PRACTICE

1. Converse: in *Ideology and its Discontents*.

2. *Voters and Elections, Past and Present*, in *Political Opinion and Behaviour* (edited by Dreyer and Rosenbaum); Wadsworth Publishing Company, Belmont, California, 1966.

3. J. Blondel: *Voters, Parties and Leaders*, pp. 75–87; Penguin, 1966.

4. R. S. Milne and H. C. Mackenzie: *Marginal Seat*; Hansard Society for Parliamentary Government, 1958.

5. Peter Pulzer: *Political Representation and Elections in Britain*, p. 102; Allen & Unwin, 1967.

6. The figures in this paragraph are derived from NOP data, analysed by Peter Pulzer, pp. 98–107.

7. See, for instance, E. A. Nordlinger: *The Working-Class Tories*, pp. 63–81; MacGibbon and Kee, 1967.

8. Blondel: *Voters, Parties and Leaders*, pp. 67–8.

9. Converse: in *Ideology and its Discontents*.

10. Nordlinger: *The Working Class Tories*, p. 151.

11. S. E. Finer, H. B. Berrington, D. J. Bartholomew: *Backbench Opinion in the House of Commons, 1955–9*; Pergamon Press, 1961.

12. Alan Watkins: *The Left*, p. 175; Anthony Blond, 1966.

13. Robert Holt and John Turner: 'Great Britain: the Labour Government and the Politics of Party Consensus,' in *European Politics II* (edited by William G. Andrews); Van Nostrand, Princeton N.J., 1968.

14. This distinction has been suggested by Professor Richard Rose in 'Parties, Factions and Tendencies,' reprinted in *Studies in British Politics*; Macmillan, 1966.

15. Finer *et al.*: *Backbench Opinion*, Chapter 4.

16. *Financial Times*, 1 June 1967.

17. J. A. Schumpeter: *Capitalism, Socialism and Democracy*; Allen & Unwin, 1954.

18. Michael Rogin: 'The American Right,' *Listener*, 8 February 1968.

19. E. J. Mishan: *The Costs of Economic Growth*; Staples, 1967.

4 / THE HARM THAT IS DONE

1. Ronald Butt: *The Power of Parliament*, p. 442; Constable 1967.

2. Butt: *The Power of Parliament*, p. 297.

3. (a) Anthony Carew: 'The Real Horror of Vietnam,' *Sun*, 25 March 1965.

3. (b) Robert Crichton: 'The Air War in Vietnam,' reprinted from *The New York Review of Books* in *New Society*, 11 January 1968.

4. Richard Pryke: *Though Cowards Flinch*; MacGibbon & Kee, 1967.

5. Richard Rose: 'The Political Ideas of Party Activists,' in *Studies in British Politics*, p. 291; Macmillan, 1966.

6. T. S. Eliot: *The Idea of a Christian Society*; Faber & Faber, 1939.

5 | ALTERNATIVE CLASSIFICATIONS

1. Converse: in *Ideology and its Discontents*.

2. H. J. Eysenck: *The Psychology of Politics*, Routledge & Kegan Paul. (Fourth Impression, 1963.) A brief account is also available in *Sense and Nonsense in Psychology*, Chapter 7; Penguin, 1957.

3. Eysenck: *The Psychology of Politics*, p. 276 *et seq.* and p. 290 *et seq.*

4. Eysenck: *The Psychology of Politics*, pp. 137-40.

5. Michael Pinto-Duschinsky: *The Political Thought of Lord Salisbury*; Constable, 1967.

6. Wittgenstein: *Philosophical Investigations*, pp. 66-7 and 76-7 (2nd edition); Basil Blackwell, 1958.

7. Eysenck: *The Psychology of Politics*, Chapter 8.

8. Eysenck: *The Psychology of Politics*, pp. 143-7.

9. See Mr Heath's suggestion in the Common Market Debate, on 9 May 1967, that the British nuclear deterrent and the French *Force de frappe* should be held as a common trust.

6 | OBSERVATIONS ON THE PARTIES

1. R. Mackenzie: *British Political Parties*; Mercury, 1964.

2. *The Treasury and Economic Policy* (second edition of *The Treasury under the Tories*), Chapter 6 (in preparation).

3. Butt: *The Power of Parliament*, p. 119.

4. See for instance H. G. Johnson, *The Economic Approach to*

Social Questions, Weidenfeld & Nicolson, 1968; Anthony Downs, *An Economic Theory of Democracy*, Harper, New York, 1958; and Donald Stokes 'Spatial Models of Party Competition', in *Elections and the Political Order*, Wiley, New York, 1966.

5. Johnson: *The Economic Approach*, p. 16.

7 / THE DILEMMA OF CHOICE

1. T. Wilson: 'The Contradiction in our Attitudes to Freedom,' *New Society*, 15 February 1968.

2. J. Grimond: *Guardian*, 5 May 1967.

3. Dingle Foot: *Hansard*, 1 December 1967, Cols. 842–50.

4. Quintin Hogg: quoted in an article by Dr David Stafford–Clark, *The Times*, 12 April 1967.

5. *The Times*, 21 October 1967.

6. *Where*, November 1967, published by the Advisory Centre for Education.

7. Sir Edward Boyle: 'Citadels of Privacy,' *Guardian*, 20 November 1967.

8. Sir Isaiah Berlin: *Two Concepts of Liberty*, Oxford, 1958.

9. T. S. Eliot: *The Idea of a Christian Society*, p. 60.

10. Eliot: *Christian Society*, pp. 16, 24, 42, 61 and 73.

11. Eliot: *Christian Society*, p. 60.

12. An account of the political attitudes of Yeats, Wyndham Lewis, Pound, Eliot and D. H. Lawrence in the context of their literary works is to be found in Martin Harrison's *The Reactionaries*, Gollancz, 1966.

13. Berlin: *Two Concepts of Liberty*.

14. Brian Barry: *Political Argument*, pp. 66, 94. Routledge & Kegan Paul, 1965.

15. Barry: *Political Argument*, p. 38 *et seq*.

8 / CONSENSUS: TRUE AND FALSE

1. Humphry Berkeley: *The Power of the Prime Minister*, Allen & Unwin, 1968.

2. Butt: *The Power of Parliament*, p. 312.

3. Butt: *The Power of Parliament*, p. 339.

4. Butt: *The Power of Parliament*, p. 315.

5. A good summary of both systems can be found in *Free Elections*, by W. J. M. Mackenzie, Allen & Unwin, 1967.

6. This case is presented by Peter Pulzer, *Political Representation*, pp. 57-8.

7. Appendix by Michael Street in *The British General Election of 1966*, p. 293.

8. See for instance, Butt: *The Power of Parliament*, Chapter 2.

9. Pulzer: *Political Representation*, p. 39.

10. This term was coined by J. Donald Kingsley in *Representative Bureaucracy*; Yellow Springs, Ohio, 1944.

11. Peter Paterson: *The Selectorate*; MacGibbon & Kee, 1967.

12. Richard Rose: 'The Political Ideas of Party Activists,' in *Studies in British Politics*, p. 285 *et seq.*; Macmillan, 1966.

13. John Rawls: 'Distributive Justice,' Chapter 3 in *Philosophy, Politics and Society*, Third series, pp. 69-72; Basil Blackwell, 1967.

INDEX